WHEN YOU CAN'T PRAY

FINBARR LYNCH SJ

First published in 2016 by Messenger Publications

Messenger Publications,
37 Lower Leeson Street, Dublin 2
www.messenger.ie

Printed in Ireland

ISBN 978-1-910248-24-9

Designed by Messenger Publications Design Department
Typeset in Centaur
Printed by Johnswood Press Ltd

MESSENGER
PUBLICATIONS
JESUITS in IRELAND

Contents

Foreword

This little book had its origins in reflection on the prayer experiences of many people, including those experiences shared during spiritual direction and directed retreats. It is also shaped by talks I gave during a Training Course for Spiritual Directors over the course of the past ten years. This course was given at the Jesuit Centre of Spirituality in Manresa House, Dollymount, Dublin 3. In the process of writing itself, many new insights came to me.

It is also the sequel to my earlier little book, entitled *When You Pray*. The significance of the title of the current book, *When You Can't Pray*, is that this one is about what happens when the Lord comes closer and gives more of himself in personal prayer. My hope is that it will be helpful to those who reach the disarming point when prayer no longer seems to work for them, hence the title.

Central to my approach to this subject of growth in prayer, is my conviction that it all begins with **baptism** when the seed of God's Trinitarian life is implanted in one's deepest centre. In baptism, we receive a share in the **Sonship** of Jesus, making us sons or daughters of God. We also receive there a share in the **prayer** of Jesus, which is his living relationship with his Father.

Something truly wonderful begins at our baptism. The seed implanted there calls to be nurtured so that it will grow into a conscious relationship with Jesus and with the Father. By God's grace, we become the **place** of Jesus' prayer and allow him full sway over our heart. We let him **pray** and also **love** in us. This is the journey that I try to describe in this little book.

I avoid, where I can, using the word '*mystical*' in describing this gift of prayer. This word comes with baggage about extraordinary phenomena, which are not central to the development of prayer. Focus on the extraordinary often makes us **lose sight** of the important truth that all this prayer is a **flowering** of the humble seed we receive at baptism. The journey is **open** to all who are baptised, and who give time to listen to the wonder of this gift that is within them. The wonder is: God's enormous desire to draw us close to him. Are we willing to respond to such a loving and personal God?

I am greatly indebted to Fr Brendan Comerford SJ, who has read every word and thought with sharp attention.

Finbarr Lynch, SJ

Part 1

WHEN YOU CAN'T PRAY

Chapter 1

The Prayer of a Sick Person

"If you want to pray, you need God,
who gives prayer to the one who prays."
(Evagrius of Pontus: *On Prayer, 59*) (*The Philokalia* I, 181)

There are many times when we experience difficulty in prayer. I want to focus on two.

There is the case of the person who has been faithful in giving time every day to personal prayer, using the gospel stories to meet Jesus and getting to know and to love him. And then a **transition** happens: the prayer becomes dry, imagination no longer helps, words are just words. One asks, "How am I to pray? Is there something wrong?"

The other case is of a person who is very sick and low in energy, and so finds it hard to sustain attention for conversation with visitors. It is the same with conversation with God. No longer is there **energy** for active prayer, or, it seems, for any prayer. Though the faith relationship with God is still alive, the energy necessary for prayer, as it was, is no longer there. Prayer has changed. How are we to make sense of this?

There is something about the prayer of the **sick** person that is akin to the prayer of a person who has experienced a **transition** from being able to pray using the imagination. In both cases, there is the feeling of helplessness, the discovery of an apparent inability to pray, and the experience of a relationship that has changed to another level. The relationship has, in fact, gone deeper, down to a level of attitude and of surrender, but it feels like a **loss**; it feels like something is wrong. In both cases, there is a letting-go happening that allows God to take charge. In both, there is a **shift** from what **I** do to what **God** is doing.

We may imagine the experience of a sick person as follows: I am in hospital, lying back in my bed. I am quite unwell. I feel it. Tests are being done on me, but no results have come back yet. Some of the tests are severe and make me feel very tired. I am not sleeping well. The delay with the results is beginning to feel ominous. I am getting the impression that my condition may be serious. I want to get well again, especially for my family's sake, but new fears are arising. I don't want to think about them, but they are not going away. I put on a good face.

My energy is very low. While I am glad that visitors are coming to see me, especially my own family, some don't realise how exhausting it is for me when they stay long. And they talk more to each other than to me. I need energy to be able to interact with them. I cannot focus for long on what they are saying to me, and my responses are meagre.

I have the same difficulty when I want to pray. It is not that God is talking to me like my visitors do, but I haven't the energy to **gather myself** together now to pray the way I used to pray. Even familiar prayers, like the Our Father, or my favourite psalm, Psalm 23, are too much of an effort now. I feel all scattered. I want to pray, but I have lost any taste I had for prayer. There is no comfort for me now in praying.

How am I to pray? Where is God for me now? I am in a very hard place; I feel caught in a bind. On the one hand, I want to get well but I am losing hope of ever being well again, and am frightened of the future. And then, on the other hand, I am trying to say 'yes' to God's will for me here, bringing myself back to the present moment, and trying to accept some mystery here. As my sister would say,

'I offer it up'. I have noted, though, that **trying to say 'yes'** to how things are does bring me a sense of **peace.** It allays my fears; it helps me to be cooperative with the nursing staff and to be interested in my family's news. That's what prayer is now for me. It is **reduced** to this: **trying to say 'yes' inside myself** to the way things are, because God must be in this somehow, even if I don't get well again. But I am not able to pray in the way I used to. Have I lost something essential?

Maybe this is okay, for I remembered something yesterday that a friend told me a good while ago. It was about a Jesuit priest named Ted, who lived for 34 years with the effects of a major stroke and was happy in himself. What struck me was that he said this man was saying 'yes' to the **limitations** brought about by the stroke, and that this 'yes' was a 'yes' to **God.** I am very conscious of my own limitations here, lying back sick in my hospital bed; even my prayer, **if** it is prayer, is so limited. I am trying to say 'yes' to **how I am**, and, at the same time, I want to get well again, if God wants that for me. I hope my 'yes' is a 'yes' to God, like it was for that man Ted. Maybe that's my prayer now. There are **no words**; but the 'yes' is in my **attitude.** I know there is **a peace** coming with it. Maybe I should say 'yes' also to this bare prayer. Often I just look at the crucifix on the wall. There's some comfort in that.

When things are quiet here, **my past** comes up. It makes me nervous about what lies ahead. But another story came back to me last night and calmed me down. It is the one about the **thief** who spoke to Jesus on Calvary, and said, 'Jesus, remember me when you come into your kingdom.' He didn't have much to his credit after a criminal past, and yet he dared to say to Jesus, 'Remember me'. I have always been struck by the response of Jesus: he promised him Paradise. 'Today with me you will be in Paradise.' I can picture the two of them going into Paradise together! I know I've got things wrong in my life; I know I could have been a better husband and father; I know I'm no saint. But Jesus will not be judging me if I **look to him**. He will be generous to me, and give me more than I deserve. After all, that thief got a **free gift**! I, too, am beginning to sense forgiveness; Jesus and I can look at each other. If I have to go, I can depend on him to look after my family. You know, my life is looking different **from this end**.

Challenges

As Thomas A'Kempis wrote in his book, *The Imitation of Christ*, "few people are improved by sickness."[1] Serious illness is quite a challenge. We can't know in advance how we will negotiate our experience of it. In the words of Enzo Bianchi, "Certainly, the ways we respond to illness are numerous, extremely varied, and impossible to foresee. We may experience dejection, rebellion, denial or bitterness." On the other hand, some possible outcomes of illness are **creative**, such as, letting-go of ego-striving, rediscovery of what is essential in life, purification of motivation, and deep acceptance of self. So we may discover the **gift** it bears for us.

"Illness," as Bianchi says, "is a **new point of view** from which to look at reality."[2] It unveils for us what our view of reality has been, stripping it of inessentials, such as, striving for riches and prestige and power. We are confronted by our creaturehood. "Illness reminds us that we have no power over life, that life is not directly available to us. It reminds us that suffering is the **fundamental question** life places before us."[3]

What meaning am I to give to my suffering? Has it no meaning? Why is this happening to me? Where am I going? This helplessness, this lack of control, can there be any good in this? As Bianchi says, "Illness does not bring with it a meaning that has already been given: on the contrary, in many respects, it destroys the meaning and purpose a person had attributed to his or her life. In our illness we are called to accept responsibility for 'assigning a meaning' to our suffering."[4]

"When Christians face illness, they find themselves called to confront the different stages that accompany their condition... to deal with reactions they may not have expected, and to reconcile their new situation with their faith... They can certainly find help and comfort in prayer and faith, but they may also find that their faith, as well as the image of God they had previously known, undergoes a **radical crisis**. As their body deteriorates, their image of God who is the Creator of the human body may fall to pieces."[5]

Where is God in this? God, who longs to draw us to him, is at work using the person's experience of helplessness to bring about surrender in love. This is an experience of **darkness**, but, "for the Christian, darkness is not the absence of God but his **concealment**."[6] God is at work.

A Gift

Not everybody is improved by illness, as A'Kempis wrote, but for the sick person who has faith in God and is prepared to engage with the puzzle of his or her experience, the helplessness in prayer can reveal a **gift** there. The gift is that **God is at work**, drawing the sick person **deeper**. The person's **lack** of energy for active prayer is God's **opportunity** to be the **active** one and draw the person deeper, down to another level, one of **attitude**, in the form of surrender or trust. The helplessness becomes a gift, the gift of **surrender** to God.

A Paradox

There is a **paradox** in the experience: what seems like failure to the sick person is **achievement** on God's part. There is helplessness at one level; God at work at another. Prayer, instead of being **done**, is now being **received**. God is the active one, and the person lets God be God. God is drawing the person into **alignment** with his will: this is a union of wills; this is prayer, even a **state** of prayer. Union with God is holiness.

Displacement
A useful word for describing what is going on is the word **"displacement"**. God is making room for Himself, so as to give us **more** of Himself and take over the praying. It is like what happens in a healthy loving relationship. There is a shift **from** "I" **to** "us", from doing things my way to wanting to please the other, from independence to relationship, from reliance on self to acknowledgement of my need of the other, from self-justification to asking forgiveness. Something that takes years for a person in his or her health to arrive at is **accelerated** for a person who is sick and willing to work on the relationship with God. It is like a crash-course, for suddenly the time is running out and God wants to use the experience of illness to bring the person closer.

The Last of the Human Freedoms
Viktor Frankl, in his famous book, *Man's Search for Meaning*, tells us that at our core level we still have a precious measure of freedom. He writes: "everything can be taken from a man but one thing: the last of the human freedoms – to choose one's attitude in any given set of circumstances, to choose one's way."[7] This is the freedom in us that God is engaging with: inviting a "yes" to himself by means of our "yes" to our circumstances; inviting surrender to him in love. At our moment of death, when we are beyond all resistance, we will let go of everything, even life itself, and let God have us. But we can practise for that moment by our "yes" to our state of illness; we can move sooner into the surrender that will eventually be drawn from us. Surrender to God is peace.

"If you want to pray, you need God,
who gives prayer to the one who prays."
Prayer is God's **gift**. Surrender to God, too, is God's gift. We can resist it. But in doing so, we will be doing a violence to our core longing for God. For in our deepest centre, there is a hollow space that only relationship with God can fill. Here, too, is the freedom that Frankl speaks of. This hollow is not an inert, empty space without movement. On the contrary, it is more like a vacuum that is alive with need for completion by an inrush of air. Conscious relationship with the mysterious, unseen God is that inrush of air. This is the gift God offers us throughout our life, and no less during our illness, no matter how bare the experience may feel. We may resist it, or we may open ourselves to it. The choice is ours: the achievement will be God's.

Encouragement

One may take encouragement from the witness of a man who was drawn into complete dependency and helplessness after a major stroke. Fr Pedro Arrupe SJ, who was then Superior General of the Society of Jesus, (the Jesuits), described in 1983 what this experience felt like for him and how he understood it:

> More than ever, I now find myself in the hands of God.
> This is what I have wanted all my life, from my youth.
> And this is still the one thing I want.
> But now there is a difference: the initiative is entirely with
>   God.
> It is indeed a profound spiritual experience
> to know and feel myself so totally in his hands.[8]

Chapter 2

Transition

"When Jesus had finished speaking, he said to Simon, 'Put out into deep water and let down the nets for a catch.'"
(*Luke* 5:4)

In the previous chapter, I described the effect that **sickness** can have on a person's experience of prayer. Lack of energy seems to render prayer impossible. Prayer has changed form; it has moved down to a level of attitude. Faith sees that God is using the person's lack of energy as an opportunity to be the active one. There is a **paradox** in the experience: the seeming failure on the person's part becomes achievement on God's part. God is, in fact, giving **more** of Himself by engaging more deeply with the person, drawing him or her into surrender and real love. The sick person is invited to make the **free choice, in faith,** of saying "yes" to how things are **as** a "yes" to God. The "yes" to God happens within the "yes" to reality. This surrender in faith is God's gift: the person cooperates.

The other case
And now let us look at the other case described in the previous chapter.

Here is a person in full health and energy. For **several years** now she has been faithful in spending time each day in personal prayer. She has learned how to hold prolonged attention on the Lord while praying with the Scriptures. She has found certain methods of prayer helpful. Using Prayer of Consideration she has learned to **reflect** on passages that speak of the Lord's care and love, and to **speak** from her heart. Use of the Ignatian method of Imaginative Contemplation has taught her how to **enter** gospel scenes using her imagination and to **meet** Jesus there and hear his love and his message. She has grown in love of her Lord and knows him as her friend. A warm, heart-felt relationship has developed. He has moved into the centre of her affections, much as happens in a growing love-relationship between a man and a woman.

Over time communication has changed. Because love has grown, prayer is now more of **heart** than of thought. Very little mental material is enough to carry her loving attention for a long time. A word, such as "come", or a phrase, such as "if you but knew the gift of God", can hold a mysterious attraction for her again and again. It has dawned on her that in prayer she is now less busy, less active, and that this must mean that God is now more active, engaging her heart and enabling the prayer. But she still needs a certain **focus** to carry her loving attention. There is a joy and ease in prayer, and a growing in-love-ness.

And then this **transition** happens. The prayer becomes **dry**. Imagination no longer helps. Words in prayer feel like "just words, words, words." Yet there is a great longing for God and for God's will. It can be a distressing change. The experience is one of disarray, loss of control, failure in prayer. Whenever she becomes quiet in order to pray and direct her heart towards God, her imagination starts moving hither and thither, instead of carrying her prayer as it used to do. Imagination is now random.

She asks herself, "What have I done to bring this about? Is there something wrong? I don't know where I am; have I gone backwards?" It feels like one is in a **trackless desert**, in unknown territory, on uncharted waters. It is new, but is it wrong? She is anxious, and wonders: "Am I being punished for something? Has God turned away from me? Where has God fled?" She doesn't know how to be in prayer. Is it prayer at all?

What has happened?

Beginnings

A broad summary of such a person's prayer – man or woman – over **many years**, might sound like this:

Looking back, I remember how attractive I found *Psalm* 139: *'O Lord, you have searched me and you know me… For you created my inmost being; you knit me together in my mother's womb… Your right hand will hold me fast.'* I was able to ruminate over this again and again. I began to feel God close and intimate. It amazed me: that my **Creator** is not only vast and mysterious, managing this whole universe, but is also closely in touch with every secret part of me. It brought me into a certain state of **wonder** that used to come upon me again whenever I saw the night sky.

I began to ask myself what is the **purpose** of my life? Why am I here? What am I made for? Where am I heading? Then, one Sunday, I heard a **homily** at Mass about God the Creator offering us all a personal relationship with Himself; that He was the one I am made for; that everything I have and everything around me is like a gift from God. So there must be a **plan** for my life. I began to understand that God is looking for my heart; that He wants to be the reason for all my choices. I began to lose a certain fear I had. I began to pray every day.

Around that time, I came across a beautiful passage in the Old Testament from the Book of *Jeremiah*: *"'I know the plans I have for you," declares the Lord, "plans to prosper you and not to harm you, plans to give you hope and a future. Then you will call upon me and come and pray to me, and I will listen to you."'* (29:11-12) I found I could think about these words and talk to God. I was getting some sense of connection during prayer. And **outside** of prayer, there was a certain peace about me, and I was more at ease with people.

A really consoling moment happened for me when I came across a few verses in *Isaiah* 43: *'I have called you by name, you are mine.'* At first, I felt a bit threatened by 'you are mine', but the words wouldn't leave me, and, after a while, I could rest in those words, and especially in words a little further on, '*Because you are precious in my sight, and honoured, and I love* **you**.' (43:1, 4) I felt good lingering over those words, though I felt unworthy. I spoke to God about my feelings.

I remember a verse from **Hosea** that intrigued me, but which I didn't understand: '*Therefore I am going to allure her; I will lead her into the* **desert** *and speak tenderly to her.*' (2:14) But now that my prayer has changed lately, I see a connection with 'desert' and I hope that God is close.

Imaginative Contemplation

Prayer became much more alive for me when I found a way to pray on the **gospel stories** about Jesus. I used to pray the Rosary and give my attention to the gospel scenes while saying the Hail Mary's, but this new way was more helpful. I was shown how to prepare myself first by getting in touch with how I was **feeling**. Then I approached God who was **waiting** for me and **looking** at me. I was able to **imagine** what was happening in the gospel scene and see the people there and hear what they were saying and even at times I became part of the scene. I noticed my **feelings** during prayer and told Jesus of my love for him and asked him to forgive me and give me patience. I had a sense of **meeting** Jesus in prayer. And my life was changing, too.

I remember sensing Jesus say to me what he said in *John 1* to Andrew and his friend, '*Come and see.*' I went with them and felt his loving gaze on me. He asked me what I wanted, and I said, 'I want to get to know you.' I found I could receive his gaze but only for a short while. It is not easy for me to let a person look at me; I feel some discomfort: what might they be seeing? Am I being judged?

Lately, I sometimes come back to a single verse in *Revelation*, chapter 3: '*Listen! I am standing at the door knocking; if you hear my voice and open the door, I will come in to you and eat with you, and you with me.*' (3:20) I thought I was the one searching for him, but it was new to see that he is waiting for my invitation. I now **begin** prayer by pausing to bring to mind that Jesus is waiting to be invited to come into my heart space. He comes as a friend. I open the door, and our eyes meet. He looks at me, not at the state my life is in. It means a lot to me that he wants to come close. It is all very simple now. I say little. It is enough just to be with him. I have become more conscious of being in a relationship with him, and of not needing to have many ideas to keep me going. The 'meal' is more like drinking a kind of atmosphere in silence. I keep going **back** to this verse. I see more in it. I am struck by the sense that he is so respectful towards me. We are like two very close friends who trust each other and don't need to say much.

Another time, I met him when I was praying over the Bartimaeus story in *Mark* 10. When he asked Bartimaeus, '*What do you want me to do for you?*' I felt he was saying this to me, and I became all warm. I was just looking at him and he at me. I felt loved. I said, 'I want to be really close to you.' I didn't know what I was asking. I saw Bartimaeus following Jesus along the way (to Jerusalem) and thought this might be his answer to me.

Another day, I had a strong impression that Jesus was saying to me what he said to Simon, '*Put out into deep water and let down the nets for a catch.*' (*Luke* 5) I felt invited to trust him and not be afraid of what might come up in my net from my past. Nothing came up, actually, but I felt I was to let go of control of my life, and go with the flow of whatever was happening. I began to accept people more and not avoid some people who were not easy to get on with.

Another time, lately, I was praying over the Transfiguration story in *Mark* 9. I had read the story beforehand and thought a bit about it, but when I came to pray on it, I couldn't get beyond the first sentence, which reads, 'After six days Jesus took Peter, James and John with him and led them up a high mountain, where they were all alone.' I was there behind Jesus and was conscious of seeing his back in some way, and I couldn't get beyond that: just being led by him and **seeing only his back**. Strangely, this kept me going for a whole week, praying for half an hour each day. The change in my prayer came soon enough after that. It is as if now I am seeing only his back.

Dare I think that this has some connection with what I read about Moses in *Exodus* 33: Then the Lord said: *'There is a place near me where you may stand on a rock. When my glory passes by, I will put you in a cleft in the rock and cover you with my hand until I have passed by. Then I will remove my hand and you will see **my back**; but my face must not be seen.'*

And then this **transition** has come. The prayer has become **dry**. It seems like nothing is happening. **Imagination** no longer helps. In fact, it is a nuisance. It is all over the place. Whenever I settle myself to pray, I have all those unsought and unwanted distractions that I can't control. Am I wasting my time here? I have lost the consoling feelings I had in prayer, and now I just have no expectation of them. What I have is an experience of helplessness, non-control, disarray. I feel a **failure** in prayer, and am tempted to give it up as a hopeless quest. I feel lost. It's like I am blind: I cannot **focus** my thoughts on God.

All I can do is **want** God, but now that is without the former feeling of consolation.

What has happened?

Before this moment of **transition** into what feels like **inability** to pray, a long and gradual development has taken place. This development has laid the foundation for the start of a **new phase** now in closeness to God. What seems like a **"wilderness"** is, in truth, a forward place, and God can speak more intimately to her **"heart"** now. She has, in fact, become more open to the Lord. The long development has laid the **foundation** for this change. On this we must reflect in the next chapter.

How to interpret?

This new but very puzzling experience is, in fact, a very good place. But unless one has heard or read about it, one could be quite thrown by it, for one's usual points of reference have been taken away. It is a crucial time for **spiritual direction** from some wise director who will help the pray-er to **interpret** what is going on, and see there what God is doing and what God now wants. The person herself knows somehow on the inside that things are probably all right, despite the disappointing experience, but she needs the outer word from someone to match that "inner word". A spiritual director will help her to see that prayer has indeed changed but not gone backwards, nor has God gone away. Prayer has moved down to a new and **deeper level**. It is the **Prayer of Faith**. Prayer is now one of **attitude**, not of mental focus. This person has been making a long inner journey that has made her ready for this new but puzzling experience. This inner journey has included her development as a person as well as her growth in prayer. She is able for a deeper relationship.

Chapter 3
Foundations

"For no one can lay any foundation other than the one that has been laid; that foundation is Jesus Christ."
(I *Cor* 3:11)

In the previous chapter, I spoke about the transition into an **imageless** prayer that can happen as part of a development in the journey of a person who has been praying for years. We traced in broad outline her **history** of prayer. And now prayer has become dry. The person feels she is in a trackless desert and is anxious; she wants so much to meet with God in prayer. A spiritual director has helped her to see that prayer has indeed changed but not gone backwards: it has changed into a new and **deeper level**. It is the **Prayer of Faith**. Prayer is now one of **attitude**, not of mental focus. This person has been making a long inner journey that has made her ready for this new but puzzling experience. This inner journey includes her growth as a person as well as her growth in prayer. It would be good to look at this journey, so as to recognise the **essential** ingredients of it.

The Journey of Prayer

A Christian's journey of prayer **begins** at baptism, and reaches its **destination** in face-to-face Vision of God. The journey passes through many phases of varying light and darkness, of willingness and reluctance, of resistance and surrender.

Christian prayer has its **roots** in the gift of **baptism**. In baptism, we are given a **share** in the Sonship of Jesus and are brought into a relationship with God as Father. We receive a **seed**, not the fully developed reality.

In order to **grow** in her given share of the Sonship of Jesus, our person needs to get to **know** Jesus, become friends with him, learn his attitudes, experience his forgiveness when she fails, but, above all, to become **like** him through frequently **meeting** him in prayer. For prayer is a meeting. She can know about Jesus through study, but to know him in a direct and intimate way she needs to meet him, meet him often, and spend time in his company. She will **meet** him in personal prayer, particularly through prayer on the gospels.

She will, of course, meet him in a special way through the Sacraments, but her meeting with him in personal prayer will dispose her for profiting as much as she can from meeting him in the Sacraments.

As baptised persons, we **share** in Jesus' relationship with God the Father. But we won't know what **shape** our own share, as daughter or son, is meant to take unless we **meet** Jesus often and get to know him. A privileged place for meeting with Jesus is in **prayer on the gospels**; this meeting **changes** us. It is like living for a long time with a family who treat each other with respect and loving attention and courtesy, and share what they have. One absorbs their ways and attitudes. One becomes **like** them. One is **changed.** Study of the gospels or any other instruction is not enough. It is by spending time in his company that we learn what **shape** our own share, as daughter or son, is meant to take. Through prayer on the gospels, I **live** with Jesus and absorb his attitudes and become like him. I meet Jesus and am **changed.**

Personal Growth

Prior to the transition to dryness in prayer, there has been a long and gradual development. It has entailed **personal growth** as well as **development in prayer.**

This person has moved **from** seeing life as concerned with LAW (duty, commandments, 'shoulds' and 'oughts', religious practices) **to** seeing life as PERSONAL RELATIONSHIP with the Lord. Duties are still fulfilled, but are now seen as part of a personal relationship, and so the focus is less on self. She is no longer a person of whim, swayed by moods; she has moved **away** from the pleasure/pain principle in her choices, and **towards** a serious commitment to values. She has become dependable and steady. She has become clearer about what is important in life: truth, people, personal integrity, love, and relationship with her God.

Her **image** of God has changed correspondingly **from** Lawgiver and Accountant **to** that of Friend. A method of prayer which she calls, **Prayer of Consideration**, has opened her to a truer perception of who God is for her: she has been mulling over some texts from the Old Testament, especially the Psalms, and now is able to hold prolonged attention on the Lord in prayer. She has met the **Loving Face** of God who surrounds her with his loving care; and she knows herself invited into a personal relationship with him. Recently, she has been meeting the **Merciful Face** of God, for she has become aware of her own faults.

But she has grown in self-esteem and self-acceptance. Somehow there is less of ego operative in her daily life, though, in truth, there is a long journey ahead for her in that regard: she has some sense of never becoming thoroughly good. She is more patient. She is less likely now to use people for her own advantage. She is able to put herself out for people, especially for her friends. They find her loyal. She is good at relating, and is able to listen. Service of others feels satisfying: "It makes me feel good to be serving."

Development in Prayer

Besides this personal growth, **prayer**, too, has developed. Personal prayer has come as a welcome discovery, and she has been giving it regular time. It has moved **from** reflecting on God's word in Scripture – her Prayer of Consideration – **to** a sense of meeting with God in relationship. She has let her reflection change how she sees herself and how she should behave towards others. This, somehow, has resulted in her finding ease in prayer. She has become grateful for her life. She has greater trust in the Lord's care of her. She is beginning to see, however, how much of ego-self there is in her motivations. She is searching for a deeper meaning to her life: what is my life really about?

When a **relationship** between two friends grows in intimacy, their way of **communicating** with each other also grows and goes through changes. Affection is felt and expressed. Touch becomes a way of communicating. The tone in which something is said speaks volumes. Words and small gestures carry more meaning. More truth is possible; trust grows; pretence is dropped; out-of-tune-ness with one another registers sharply. Disagreements are aired. Yet the desire to please the other is stronger. There is a sense of **depth** in the relationship.

The same goes for **prayer**. As she and God draw closer and deeper, how she and God are **communicating** also changes. Feelings come to the surface and are expressed. The sense of touch picks up something of God's active presence, for touch is the primary sense, the first sense alerted in the newborn child. Feelings become honest. Resistance to God raises its head, but she brings it to prayer. She is becoming more realistic about herself. It becomes easier to be present to the Lord in loving attention. Less material carries longer attentiveness. She has grown in her desire to please the Lord. Prayer, somehow, seems deeper.

And then comes this change in prayer!

Spiritual Director

A spiritual director, hearing her story, will keep this background of development in mind.

- ❦ He/she will try to **situate** this moment of change in prayer in the person's **history** of prayer.
- ❦ He/she will also try to pick up on what **growth** has happened for the person **outside** of prayer.

Has the foundation been laid?

For the inside and the outside must **match**. Prayer and lifestyle **interact**. Prayer is as deep or as shallow as the person has become.

A Shortcut?

An induced or **acquired** quietening in prayer by means of a **method**, such as the use of a mantra, or the practice of Centering Prayer or of the Jesus Prayer, can do harm if a **build-up** of felt knowledge of Christ and of growth in virtue has not been put in place. There is quite a difference between use of a mantra at the beginning of prayer to steady an unruly mind and using a mantra as a method throughout the whole time of prayer. It takes a **long time** to grow into the mind of Christ and to break down the habit of selfish living. If simplification in prayer is brought on by a prayer method **before** the enriching **foundation** of faith knowledge and personal growth has been laid, the person may find he or she is in a silent prayer that really is narcissistic, turned in on self, "a resting in oneself rather than a transcendent outreach to God."[9] Without such a foundation, a word, such as "come", or a phrase, such as "if you but knew the gift of God," will carry no meaning that can be expressive of loving attention. They will be empty, and without any resonance in the heart. "The human heart needs to be **prepared** before it is fit for habitual contemplative prayer" – prayer without images. "An important part of that preparation is the **actual following of Christ in daily life** – what meditation [i.e. reflective prayer, nourished by the Scriptures] is very much about, as we have seen." [10]

A Gift of Grace

The quietening in prayer that comes upon a person in the form of dryness **after** this long preparation is a **gift of grace**, not a human acquisition. This dryness is not parched earth. It is what St John of the Cross calls "an act of general, loving, peaceful, and tranquil knowledge, drinking wisdom and love and delight." [11]

Readiness

A foundation has been laid in this person's relationship with the Lord. She is ready to hear that God has not gone away and that prayer has not disappeared but has descended to another level.

She has moved **from** relating with the Lord through the level of the **senses** (words, images, surface feelings) **to** relating **without** the senses: this is the level of **faith**. Words, images and surface feelings are still there but in an unfocused way; the imagination is random for the person is awake; but these are not carrying the connection with God that is prayer. On one level, the surface level, there are distractions: but the prayer is not there, for it is at the **deeper** level in the form of desire for God, a wanting of God, a surrender to what God wants. Prayer is now an **attitude**, not a mental focus.

Ignatian Imaginative Contemplation

Since I have referred many times to this way of praying, I would like to speak more directly about it.

Methods of prayer fall into two categories, broadly speaking:

> ❦ **Imageless**, self-emptying prayer, such as Centring Prayer, Christian Meditation (use of a mantra), The Jesus Prayer.

> ❦ Prayer **with images**; use of all the faculties. I use my **imagination** to help me **see, hear, feel** in prayer on a gospel story. I use my **mind** to reflect, and my **will** to desire and love. I become fully involved.

Prayer with the use of my imagination and all my faculties is very profitable for laying down a precious **foundation** in preparation for the level of prayer known as **Prayer of Faith**. Ignatius did not invent this way of praying; it was already in the tradition. But he gave it a more definite shape in his *Spiritual Exercises*.

In Gospel Contemplation, as taught by Ignatius, "we let the **words** of a gospel scene touch our **imaginations**, much as poetry or a novel might, asking the Lord to **reveal** himself to us in the process." **Ignatius** believed that if we let our imaginations go in this way, God will **reveal** to us who Jesus is. We will **meet** Jesus, and learn more from the meeting than we would learn from study. Study tells us **about** Jesus; meeting him in prayer gives us a different kind of knowledge, an **intimate**, heart-felt knowledge.

In this kind of prayer, I let myself **see** the persons, **hear** what they say or may say, **observe** what they are doing, and then **reflect** on how this concerns me and my own story. I explore the scene and allow it to open up for me. As, for instance, the scene on the storm at sea in Matthew 8:23-27, adapting the words of Timothy Gallagher in his book, *An Ignatian Introduction to Prayer:*[12]

I imagine I am at the lakeside as Jesus gets into the boat. I **see** the disciples following him into the boat. This is my heart's desire also — to follow the Lord, to be with him, and not let fear hold me back.

I am **with them** in the boat as we set out. All is peaceful. I **watch** as Jesus, wearied by his day of service to so many people, falls asleep in the stern of the fishermen's boat; Jesus is a man like us in all things but sin.

And now, with the disciples, I become aware that the **wind** is rising, the **waves** increasing. I watch these fishermen: their **words**, their **faces**, tell me beyond doubt that now we are in serious danger. I **hear** their cries of panic. I **feel** the power of the wind, I **hear** the crashing of the waves, I **see** the water pouring into the boat.

I am **reminded** of the storms in my own life, in the past, and even now. Suddenly, everything seems **out of control**, headed towards darkness. I feel **fear** rise in my heart. All human means are exhausted, and the fear remains.

And Jesus sleeps. I **see** the men draw near to Jesus, as the boat rolls and pitches, tossed by the storm. And, **with them**, I too cry out: 'Lord, save us! We are going down.' I know this fear, born of a heart filled with fear.

Jesus awakens, and, *before he intervenes*, says to them, and to me: '**Why are you terrified, O you of lit-**

tle faith?' I **hear** Jesus ask this question of me, personally: Why are you afraid? And, slowly, from my heart, I answer. I **tell** the Lord of the storms in my life, of the storms in my heart, of the fears that burden me.

And I **hear** his invitation to have faith in him, to trust.

Now, they, and I with them, **watch** Jesus stand, and with a word, order the wind and the sea to be calm. With amazement, we **hear** the wind die, we **watch** the sea grow calm. We know that all danger is past.

Now I am **alone with Jesus.** I **speak** to him of the power I have witnessed in him, and of the ease with which he can calm the storms in my life, in my heart. I, too, marvel at the power in him. I **speak** to him from my heart.

This is a **sample** of what Ignatius wants us to do:

Ignatius encourages us to SEE, to LISTEN, and to CONSIDER what the people in the scene are doing. This helps us to **enter** into the heart of the gospel message. It **opens us up** to a very personal **discovery** of what God might want to reveal to us. We aren't just observers standing back. Instead, we draw close; we make ourselves **present.** The invitation is to be a **participant,** to be **involved** in the scene, actually part of it.

There are **two ways** of being close to the scene: one way is by **watching** the scene closely, as an observer; the other is by imagining myself as a **character** in the scene.

> ❦ I **look** long and lingeringly on each of the gospel characters.
> ❦ I **listen** to what they are saying or might be saying.
> ❦ I **consider** what they do.

And each time I **look** or **listen** or **consider** what people are doing, "I will reflect on this to draw some profit from what I see... from their words... from what I have noted."[13] By this kind of reflection, Ignatius means that I **let myself** be touched, or enlightened, or changed. He means that when I look or listen or consider what people are doing, I am to **let God act on me** in some way; I let God give me a **response** to the gospel. God takes the **initiative** in my personal prayer on the gospels, and I **let myself** be affected. It may be an insight I am given, or a touch of love, and guidance towards a decision. If the person is able to let herself be affected like this, it lays the foundation for the letting-go that will later be invited in prayer of faith.

My response

It would only be natural to **speak** with the Lord about what has been going on in the prayer time. If this hasn't happened **during** the time, I make sure to speak with him at the **end,** before I take my leave of him. If something has struck me notably, then that is most likely what I will be talking of. However, if **nothing** seems to have happened for me, I bring that very fact to the Lord and say **how I feel about that** — maybe disappointed, or frustrated, or asking why. I **share** with the Lord, as one friend does with another. If **I have** received something, I will **thank** him. But sometimes my sharing with the Lord will **not** be in words, but, instead, will just be a **being-with** Jesus or God or the Spirit.

Meeting Jesus in prayer: what does this mean?

I have said we use our imagination in prayer on the gospels in order to **meet** Jesus.

But **how** can this be? It is **by faith.**

What is faith? Faith is **connectedness.** I have faith, so I am connected with Jesus now in a **living relationship** with him. Jesus is risen and alive, and is in a **living relationship** with me now — two living persons **connected** with each other. There is a **bond** of connectedness between us. I have no such connection with historical characters, such as Plato or Shakespeare.

All Jesus' **human experiences** are still alive in him. Remember that he appeared on Easter Sunday evening to his disciples still **bearing his wounds** in his risen body. So I can **connect** with him by calling to mind in prayer any of his human experiences.

For instance, even though the Nativity of our Lord happened at one particular moment in history, I can connect now with him **and** those events because he is present to me **now** with all his human experiences. I can **call to mind** his tiny body and be in **wonder** at the humility of my God who has chosen to be born one like us.

It is as if the gap of **historical time** does not matter. **My faith,** alive in me, means that I have this living connection **now** with Jesus. I can connect with him speaking with the woman at the well; I can contemplate him hanging on his cross for me. So when I meet him in prayer and call to mind **any part** of his life story, I become **present** to his story: and Jesus, being alive, becomes **present** to me.

Jesus **meets me** through **my remembering in faith.**

Chapter 4

Beyond the Beginnings

"Therefore, I will now allure her, and bring her into the wilderness, and speak to her heart."

(*Hosea* 2:14)

In the previous chapter, I described the inner journey of personal growth coupled with growth in prayer. This has laid the strong foundation for the important change of level in prayer known as Prayer of Faith. Our pray-er has grown in a measure of personal maturity; there is less of ego-self operative in her dealings with others. In personal prayer, she has encountered the Risen Jesus many times. In prayer, she has also tasted her own mixture of welcome and unwelcome feelings and has experienced a certain education of feelings through bringing them to the Lord. She has grown in a loving friendship with him, and now cannot do without him in her life. She is more realistic about herself, less demanding of others, and more generous in her love.

A New Journey

Mary Magdalene had been cured of some very severe malady by Jesus, described as "seven demons" in *Luke* 8:2. Grateful for such liberation, she joined the group of women who travelled around with Jesus and his twelve disciples. She came to know him intimately through watching him and listening to him. He became the centre of her life. She knew what it was to hold him and be held by him. Her love was profound. This made her strong in herself, strong enough to be present to him at Calvary.

On the Sunday morning, **Jesus is risen**. Mary is one of those women looking for his body to complete the anointing, a final gesture of her care and love. She is at the tomb, distraught; he should be here, and she can't find him. His death itself already feels like a profound loss, but now, this complete disappearance is more than she can bear. What has happened? She lingers aimlessly at the tomb, not knowing what to do. Her one desire is to see him again, the Jesus she knew, even his dead body. This tomb is where it should be. So much has been taken from her already. And now the one she loves is utterly gone. She feels empty, and lost.

Then Jesus, now risen, gradually reveals that he is not the gardener but the one who knows and loves Mary. He speaks her name, "Mary". She knows this voice and she is sure it is he. Her immediate response is to embrace him: she is trying to **recapture the past**. But Jesus is risen: he is **changed**. So he says, **"Do not cling to me."** *(John* 20:17*)* He asks her to desist from her attempt to re-establish the relationship she once had with him. An entirely **new** situation is being established: it is even **better. She is invited into resurrection faith**, to accept that Jesus is with the Father. No wonder he says, "Do not cling to me." It is as if he is saying, "Let go: let **me** cling to you, instead. Let me be **inside** you, more intimate than ever before, filling you with my presence, my prayer, my union with my Father, my awe, my love."

Mary has begun **a new journey**. This is **our** journey, too.

"Therefore, I will now allure her."

Our praying person has been allured by the Lord to give him more of her heart in prayer and in daily life. The intimacy has grown to such an extent that **very little** mental material was enough to hold her in prolonged loving attention on her Lord.

"I found I was held for a long time in prayer by phrases like, 'Here I am', and 'Jesus touched them', and even by words like 'precious' and 'all'. I noticed that the **fascination** I felt with the word or phrase was much greater and wider than the **meaning** of the words. These were like a **contact-point**, linking me to something mysterious. It was as if the word or phrase was in the **foreground** of my attention, and I was aware at the same time of a distant **horizon**."

If she had been able to reflect further on her experience, or if she had brought it to her spiritual director, she might have noted a **disproportion** here between how long her loving attention was being held and how little mental focus enabled this to happen. And then she might have seen that God was causing this by playing a **more active** part in her prayer, and allowing her to be **receptive and restful**. God was mysteriously at work, alluring her, pouring delicate love into her, and winning her heart. It is this allurement by God that allows prayer be **simple** like this: very little activity in the person **revealing** that God is clearly at work. God is drawing close.

"And bring her into the wilderness."

But now she is about to face into **a new situation**. The Lord wants to move closer still. He will do this by bringing her into "the wilderness", where she will be deprived of the consolations of her simplified prayer, and there be given the deeper closeness of **resurrection faith**.

Mary Magdalene's path to full resurrection faith was through the bitter experiences of watching the rejection, suffering and death of her Beloved, and losing the intimacy she once had. The scooping out of her ego-self was not the end: it created in her a capacity to receive the Risen Jesus in a new and deeper way. The experience was a terrible transition that only her great love for him could bear. It was a short and sharp journey.

Our praying person also has such a journey before her, but it is likely to be **spread out** over a long space of years; the Lord will gradually move closer and make her able for close union with himself. She will be brought into the "wilderness" of not having the **felt consolations** to which she had become accustomed.

"There are days when I find I can't focus on the Lord the way I used to. And then there are other days when the focus on him is easy again. I began to know I should to be in prayer whatever the experience might be, for I knew he deserves my time, at least."

After several experiences of less satisfying prayer, **a definite transition occurs**, and it takes the form of a persistent **dryness** in prayer. It is a **Prayer of Faith**. Neither words nor images are able now to carry the prayer relationship. **Words** in prayer feel like "just words, words, words." They have lost their power to hold the person in loving attention. **Thoughts**, too, are of no help in prayer. She can't focus her attention. **Feelings**, also, have become dried up. Prayer feels like being in a cinema, but one doesn't know where the screen is. **Imagination** is random, moving hither and thither, because the prayer is beneath it; it is random and active because one is awake, but it is no longer carrying the prayer.

Prayer is now **desire**, love, a wanting of God, a wanting to surrender to God. So, a strong desire for God and for God's will is still at work in her, but it carries with it no sense of satisfaction during prayer. She is like the Beloved in the *Song of Songs*, crying: "I sought him whom my soul loves; I sought him, but found him not; I called him, but he gave no answer." (*Song of Song* 3:1 RSV) She is very conscious of what she has lost in experience.

This **transition** is a difficult time. The **experience** of prayer is one of helplessness, non-control, disarray. There is **anxiety** about the prayer itself: "Have I gone wrong somewhere?" There is anxiety about doing God's will in general: "How can I please him?" There is a sense of failure in prayer, and a temptation to give it all up as a hopeless effort. One's **imagination** is all over the place when one sets oneself to pray, and these distractions are unsought and unwanted. One cannot focus one's thoughts on God. All one can do is focus one's **desire** on God, **want God**, but this is without the former consolations of God. Efforts to return to earlier fervour in prayer by, say, Gospel contemplation, all end in failure. Nevertheless, the longing for God and the things of God continues, but one doesn't understand what is happening, and why. A **mantra**, said however **without feeling**, can allay the imagination's wanderings, like the way one would slow down a swinging candelabrum by a succession of slight touches at the edge of each swing. The gentle use of a mantra does quieten the flotsam and jetsam of surface awareness, but the mantra doesn't carry prayer, and feeling should not be put into the mantra, for feeling would lift you off the level where God is actively at work.

The prayer is at a level below the surface feelings. **Prayer is now in the desire for God.**

Prayer has shifted down into **attitude and desire**, such as, desire to be with Jesus; the attitude of wanting to do God's will; the desire to be unselfish. It is a shift to the **level of will**, which is deeper than that of feelings; it is a shift to commitment, to self-sacrifice.

Any attempt to **focus** in prayer seems to interfere with the relationship: in order to be **in contact** with God, she needs to be **out of contact** with anything definite; she must let go; she must float.

The **imagination** – and hence the ability to think – cannot now contribute. The imagination becomes random, and it occupies itself with all sorts of flotsam and jetsam. Its waywardness can take away one's satisfaction in prayer, but it is not actually preventing prayer. It takes a very long time to come to terms with this.

At a deeper level, she is being engaged by God. There are **two levels**. This is now **a received prayer**. God is presenting himself as spirit to the spiritual faculties – intellect and will – and is by-passing the imagination.

Aridity, or dryness, is the **pain** experienced by the person whose imagination, with its words and images, tries in vain to participate in the prayer which is happening below the level of her senses. Images and words and surface feelings have been part of her prayer all along, so now the sense level is **in pain** at being excluded from the focus on the Lord. It feels kept in the dark, as it were. The pain will continue until the person learns to **submit** to what the Lord is doing. The Lord is by-passing the imagination to engage more deeply with her.

With all this newness, one feels that one has gone backwards. This is a crucial stage for spiritual direction. The praying person needs affirmation, the assurance that all is well.

"And speak to her heart."

The Lord has not gone away. He has drawn **closer** to her and is speaking to her heart, but she doesn't realise this yet.

She resembles Mary Magdalene at the tomb, being addressed in all kindness by Jesus, now risen, but not recognising him at first. He speaks of a new way of being present. Her old ideas of presence, connectedness and intimacy are not adequate now for this new stage in her friendship with him. So he says, "Do not cling to me." He will make Mary aware of a deeper level in herself where she and he will meet. He will transform her, giving her a share in his own dispositions.

In what way is the Lord speaking to the **heart** of this person experiencing dryness in prayer? We can say that God is **giving**, and God is **drawing**.

God is **giving**. St John of the Cross teaches us that God is **giving** "a secret inflow of the loving wisdom of God."[14] He says in *The Dark Night*: "For **contemplation** is nothing else than a secret and peaceful and loving inflow of God, which, if not hampered, fires the soul in the spirit of love."[15] God is giving himself as **love** and as **wisdom**. His love draws her will, which is her capacity for love, and his wisdom addresses her mind, bringing her into the mystery of himself. God's action is "secret" because the senses — what we usually use for knowing — cannot perceive what God is doing and are not directly involved in it. It is an "inflow" because it is all God's doing, so she is simply to receive.

God is **drawing**. Through the Prophet Jeremiah, God told his Chosen People, "If you seek me with all your heart, I will let you find me, says the Lord." (*Jer.* 29:13-14 NRSV) And now God is saying to this person, "Come to me in prayer with all your heart; come without self-interest; **come to me for myself**, not for my gifts, and I will let you find **me** in a new way. I am greater than my gifts. So, come without an eye to what satisfaction you may get for yourself."

At this stage, in this difficult experience of dryness in prayer, God is **drawing** her into a greater unselfishness in prayer, and, in the process, is drawing her down to a deeper level in herself. At this level, she wants to be here for God more than for herself. **Time** is now her sacrificial lamb, as it were; she puts it beyond usefulness to herself and spends it on God's terms. It is God she wants, and God she wants to please. This is the **attitude** that St Ignatius expresses in the "Preparatory Prayer", in his *Spiritual Exercises*, #46, and throughout the *Exercises*. In paraphrase, it goes like this: "I ask for the grace that all that I do and all that happens in me may be **directed purely to the service and praise of the Divine Majesty.**" This attitude places me in my fundamental truth before God, for I am made **for** God; so whatever he wants, I want. This attitude is God's gift.

The Experience

Prayer is dry. I **want** God. But I don't **feel** this act of my will. I know I want God and yet I don't feel it. I am **giving** myself to God in my prayer, and also in my choices outside of prayer. I know I love God, but I don't feel this love anymore. This is a new experience for me. Why is this possible?

My imagination flies about. I can't focus my attention on God in prayer. I seem to be wasting time, and idle. I can't feel that I actively want God and God's will. But on reflection afterwards, I perceive that I am really **intensely active**: for it is my desire for God, my desire to be there for God that keeps me sitting in a prayer that feels like a waste of time. What is going on in this prayer has to be beyond a level where I see and feel.

Dom John Chapman writes:

> ...while our will is making its intense (but almost imperceptible) act of love, our imagination is running about by itself, just as it does in a dream; so that we **seem** to be full of distraction, and not praying at all. But this is the contrary of the fact. The distractions, which are so vivid to us, are not **voluntary** actions, and have no importance; whereas the **voluntary** action we are performing is the **wanting** God, or giving ourselves to God.
>
> ...the **real prayer** is the **act of the will** (wanting, loving, etc.) behind all this. You cannot **feel** this act

of the will; but you can know it. What you **feel** is in the lower part of the soul (imagination, emotion) and does not matter; the activity of the higher part of the soul you do not **feel**, but you **know** it. You may **feel** distracted, despondent, miserable, or you may **feel** full of love or desire; but all this is unimportant. What matters is the act of the will (which you **know** but do not **feel**) which accepts all these feelings from God, and gives you to Him to be his, and (accepts) to have and to be only what He wills. We have to learn to live by the higher part of our soul, and pay no attention to anything else.[16]

Prayer has shifted to a deeper level in us, which Chapman — and many others — refers to as a "higher part of our soul", where our spiritual faculties of intellect and will reside. This level is deeper within our being. My prayer now is desire. Each time my desire for God is activated, I am praying. In the words of St Augustine,

"Longing is always praying, though the tongue be silent.
If one is ever longing, one is ever praying." (*Sermones*, 80, 7)

Preparation for prayer

This Prayer of Faith is now below the level of ideas and images; it is a received prayer; and so, any **deliberate thinking** obstructs full prayer. She cannot now be in full prayer while using a gospel scene or the words of a psalm. So how is she to **prepare** for prayer?

I asked my spiritual director about this, and I was told: 'Your preparation for prayer is in **how you live** outside of prayer. Your attitudes, and the choices you make, in your daily life, are what you bring to prayer. They **dispose** you for prayer, or **impede** your prayer. How you are **in your heart** is your preparation.'

So prayer and life seek to become integrated. This will be a topic for the next chapter.

Chapter 5

Facing into Darkness

"Then the Lord said (to Moses), 'There is a place near me where you may stand on a rock. When my glory passes by, I will put you in a cleft in the rock and cover you with my hand until I have passed by. Then I will remove my hand and you will see my back; but my face must not be seen.'"
(*Exodus* 33:21-23) (NIV)

In the previous chapter, I described the simplified prayer of a person who has grown in loving friendship with her Lord. The intimacy has grown to such an extent that only a little mental material is enough to hold her in prolonged loving attention on her Lord. This development is revealing that God is playing a more active part in her prayer.

But now a change takes place: God's action comes deeper still. God engages with her **below** the level of mental focus or images or surface feelings. God draws her into **resurrection faith**. God descends to the level of her desire for God, so now there is a new depth in the relationship. But the **experience** of prayer feels like a "wilderness"; it is one of dryness and helplessness and disarray. She has lost the felt consolations to which she had become accustomed, for a definite **transition** has taken place. Prayer has shifted into **desire** and **attitude**. It is at a different level. It feels like one has gone backwards. "Has something gone wrong?" she asks. It is a very difficult time for her. It is her love for God that keeps her coming before him in prayer. She is, in fact, receiving more of God. Gradually, she will recognise the **two levels** in her prayer and perceive the gift.

This is a crucial stage for spiritual direction.

In this chapter, I want to linger for a while over the initial experience of this transition into the dryness of the Prayer of Faith. It is a difficult time. How am I to negotiate it? What gift does it bear for me? How am I to grow in my relationship with God? What is its impact upon my daily life?

But first let us consider **Moses** who is told he may see only God's **back**. It reminds us of the darkness of the Prayer of Faith. Moses was at prayer. He was in a space reserved for prayer called the "Tent of Meeting". He was in intimate communion with the Lord. He wanted more of God.

"Then Moses said, 'Now show me **your glory.**'" (*Exodus* 33:18)

But the Lord said that this would be too much for Moses to bear as no human being would survive the full-on encounter with God's glory. What God **will** reveal to Moses is his goodness, compassion, mercy and faithfulness. (cf. 34:5-7)

"And the Lord said, 'I will cause **all my goodness** to pass in front of you... But', he said, 'you cannot see my face, for no one may see me and live.'" (33:19, 20)

However, the Lord will let Moses see his **back**:

"Then the Lord said to Moses, 'There is a place near me where you may stand on a rock. When my glory passes by, I will put you in a cleft in the rock and cover you with my hand until I have passed by. Then I will remove my hand and you will see **my back**; but my face must not be seen.'" (33:21-23)

Moses is given to understand that to see the Lord's **back** is a most intimate communion with him. **This darkness is the Lord's intimate presence.** Moses will learn all the goodness of the Lord through how the Lord deals with his own people, but **intimate communion** will be dark, like seeing the Lord's back.

Our pray-er has been brought into a prayer of **faith**. It is not like having clear face-to-face vision. It is **dark**, like seeing someone's **back**, with no features discernible. Who is this mysterious one? Am I really present to someone? It is more like seeing someone in a fog: someone is there, but perception is very vague. Vague it may be as an experience, but this meeting with the Lord is **intimate communion.** One is more conscious of what one has lost of one's former experience of prayer than of gain. It takes time and unselfishness to appreciate that one has been given a precious gift.

This is a crucial time for spiritual direction, so as to be reassured that one has moved forward, and not backward. One also needs to learn how to deal with what appear to be distractions. What am I to make of the new awarenesses that come to me? How am I to prepare for prayer?

Moses is also given another gift, which is relevant to our subject. While communing with the Lord in the Tent of Meeting, he asked the Lord for whatever he would need as leader of the Lord's people:

> Moses said to the Lord, 'You have been telling me, 'Lead these people,' but you have not let me know whom you will send with me... If you are pleased with me, teach me your ways so I may know you and continue to find favour with you.' The Lord replied, **'My Presence** will go with you, and I will give you rest.' (*Exodus* 33:12-14)

Or, as another translation renders it, "**I myself** shall go with you and I shall give you rest." (NJB)

Our pray-er has been brought into a prayer, not only of darkness, but of **presence**. It bears God's **promise** to be with her. The Lord himself has opened a space in her which is rooted in the gift of Baptism. Eventually, by God's grace and her sacrificial love, she will become aware of carrying her Lord's own prayer in her; she will become the **place** for his prayer; she will become a temple, a well.

Preparation for prayer

My director said: "Your preparation for prayer now is in how you live **outside** of prayer."

> The self I bring to prayer is the same self that I am **outside** of prayer. It is important now that prayer and daily living become matched. Prayer now is desire. Desire for God **inside** of prayer must be

matched by desire for God **outside** of prayer. One must **want** God's will and also **do** God's will. Desiring God in prayer is going to reveal my out-of-tuneness with God in how I am living. Though the experience of prayer is dark, seeing, like Moses, God's back, as it were, there is a kind of **light** that shines back upon me to show me my lack of love, and what God's will is for me. Not only will I learn about myself, but like Moses, I will learn much also about God. I will learn how good God is. I will learn his faithful love, his compassion and mercy. God is revealing himself, and also me, in this dark prayer.

Let us look first at the **experience** of this prayer, and then at how it **impinges** upon my life.

Managing the prayer: Are there Distractions?

How am I to manage prayer itself? Prayer is dry. It feels like self-gift but without echo. I am trying to be present to God on God's terms. The helplessness I experience is forcing me to let God be in control of how prayer happens. This is not easy.

The imagination – and hence the ability to think – cannot now contribute, for contact with God in full prayer is no longer at this level now. Nevertheless, when I set myself to pray, I find my imagination is random, occupied with all sorts of thoughts and images. This is just the way it happens: those distractions are unsought and unwanted. It bothers me. I **trust** that they are not spoiling my prayer. My director tells me that my prayer, my connection with God, is **below** that level of involuntary distractions: these are simply part of being awake. Because one is awake, he says, the imagination needs and seeks some focus, and so it becomes random, and it occupies itself with all sorts of flotsam and jetsam, while, at a deeper level, one is being engaged by God. For this is a received prayer: here God is the active one. God is presenting himself as spirit to the spiritual faculties of intellect and will, and **by-passing** the imagination. So, the prayer is somewhere else. It is hard to make the transition to allowing God to be the agent in prayer. After years and years of contributing to prayer and making the effort to be attentive and taking responsibility for it, I am now unable to manage myself the way I used to. But my director tells me that all is well and that I am to be perfectly satisfied to have that shifting surface awareness. This sounds strange.

The director quotes Dom John Chapman:

As distractions, when involuntary, do not spoil our prayer, and when merely of the imagination scarcely even disturb it, we ought to be perfectly satisfied to have them. We are not to be resigned to them, but more — to will them; for a contemplative is never to be resigned to God's Will, but to will It. The result of this practice will be to decrease distractions by decreasing worry. If we only want God's Will, there is no room for worry. [17]

I am to **will** this state of surface awareness, while below this I desire God. I am to want this state. For this is a contemplative prayer. He teaches me that a contemplative is never to be merely **resigned** to God's will, but to **will** It, that is, to want It.

Upstairs, Downstairs

A story may help. A woman is downstairs. Her two children, Mary and John, aged 4 and 2, are upstairs at play. A visitor comes to the door and knocks: it is Jesus. She welcomes him into the parlour downstairs and gives him her full attention. They look at one another. No word is spoken, but there is a sense of presence to each other. She wants to be with him, and he with her. Upstairs the children are running about. She hears their voices, knows which door is now being shut. As a mother, she knows exactly what they are about while she continues to stay attentive to her guest. If she wants to quieten the children, she has to abandon her guest to do so; if she wants to stay with her guest, and this is what she wants to do, she has to put up with the noise upstairs.

The imagination is now like those children: it will not stay quiet. The "distractions" that engage the surface mind now are only **accompanying** her presence to the Lord in prayer, but are not blocking her prayer, for the prayer is downstairs in the parlour, as it were.

They are **not** truly distractions, for she does not allow them to take her away from her guest.

Prayer is desire for God

Desire for God in prayer is not helped by any attempt to focus one's mind or imagination on God. A favourite verse of Scripture will not be of help. Prayer is not carried by any mental focus, for God is now present to the person at a level **below** mental focus. We are talking here about the experience of **full** prayer. If one does use an image or a word, it is like turning the tap only half-on. But for **full** prayer, one can only focus one's **desire** or one's **attitude**: to want God's will; to submit to what is happening in this prayer because this is what God is allowing; to be here on God's terms; to wait on God; to stay the time; to let this time be beyond usefulness to oneself, for the sake of relationship with God; to be like a donkey, as it were, because nothing else works anyway. There is surrender here, but without the ease in surrender that will come later.

Dom John Chapman teaches:

> One must accept joyfully and with the whole will exactly the state of prayer, which God makes possible for us here and now; we will to have that, and no other. It is just what God wills for us. We should **like** to be rapt to the third heaven; but we

will to be as we are, dry, or distracted, or consoled, as God wills.

It is just the same **out** of prayer. We may wish for a great many things – for a good dinner, or for more suffering, or the prayer of quiet – without any imperfection, provided these are involuntary wishes. But we **will** only what we have, what God's providence has arranged for us – only no sin, we repeat, only no **imperfection**.[18]

Why must I say "yes" to these "distractions" that are irrelevant to this Prayer of Faith? Why can't I be aware only of my Lord in this prayer? I would like to give him my pure, undistracted attention. Why must I say "yes" to the random behaviour of my imagination? Am I not to try to control it?

The reason for my "yes" to my non-control is that in this way I am saying "yes" to the way I am made. I am an embodied spirit; I am inextricably a composite of body and spirit. When God chooses to engage with me in a way that by-passes my imagination, God does not disempower my imagination or take it away. I am awake; my imagination is still functioning. So, I am to accept this. In accepting the disarray of my imagination, I am accepting God. In allowing myself to be unable to control my imagination, I am letting God be in control. This is surrender to God; it is worship and love. God is honoured.

Concern about these surface awarenesses keeps being a bother to praying people; it is hard to accept fully the accompaniment of surface awareness in Prayer of Faith.

Chapman mentions "imperfection" above: what does he mean? I quote:

To show you what I mean, I will point out that this contemplative prayer **stops dead** when we (by a wilful imperfection) refuse what God asks of us. That is to say, when we are **not** giving our will to God.[19]

He is speaking of wilful imperfection.

Prayer and Life

Growth in contemplative prayer is an aspect of the person's growth **outside** of prayer. Prayer will not be helped now by technique — the time for techniques is past. What matters now is cooperation with the Lord **within** prayer, by allowing my state of awareness to be just as it is. The effort **outside** of prayer is to be Christ-like in relation to other people and to one's tasks in life. The growth of the prayer hinges very definitely on the growth in oneself as a person; development in the prayer will be the **echo** of the development in being; what matters is the kind of person you become.

Shadow-side

Let us look at what is happening to our person who has entered the Prayer of Faith. Not only has prayer itself become an experience of helplessness and non-control, but **outside of prayer** a new awareness arises: it is of one's shadow side. One becomes painfully aware of how poor one's love is. One asks, "Is this why my prayer has changed and become difficult? I am sinful. I feel distanced from God. But I feel a need for God more than ever. I feel anxiety now, whereas before I was confident of my goodness."

What has happened? The Lord's new closeness at the level of one's desire for God in this Prayer of Faith is shining **new light** into one's consciousness. This light is itself invisible, like white light is, but what it shines on is what is revealed, and this sight is painfully unwelcome. It is like being confronted by the sight of dust on the desktop and the cobwebs in the corner when the sun shines in; they were there already but are now revealed. One perceives **more** of the love that is coming in from God, revealing what is not love. One sees so much **self-interest** in one's dealings with others.

"How insincere I am! I see myself looking for notice, drawing attention to myself, being competitive in conversation, seeking approval, wanting to be the centre of attention. I feel jealous of others who seem better; I measure myself by comparing myself with others; I feel put down if someone doesn't notice me. I notice feelings of intolerance and superiority. I am ready to exclude somebody." One feels like St Peter in his fishing boat when he has seen into the depths of Jesus and says, "Go away from me, Lord, for I am a sinful man," unworthy of you. (*Luke* 5:8)

Deeper
This dark experience goes even **deeper**. Happenings that seemed manageable some years ago are now acutely painful; the disparaging remark from someone about one's qualifications or one's family background now cuts through to the quick. One can recognise that there is an obvious **disproportion** between what was said and how one felt about it. This disproportion indicates that unfinished business from the past is surfacing so as to be befriended and then healed by the Lord. I must let the hurt be felt. But what else must I do? I must **look** to the Lord to give me the approval I am looking for so as to cope with the disapproval I have experienced from my colleague in the office.

This new sensitivity to hurt is not unrelated to the new vulnerability to the Lord's loving presence that has been developing. But the extra pain has come up from an issue in the past.

Childhood
In our childhood, we grow up experiencing three basic instinctual needs, those for enough **security**, enough **approval**, and enough **power or control**. **Enough** security, approval and power afford us a degree of happiness, and enable us to grow up with a sense of personal worth, and a confidence that we can cope well with our existence. However, a **lack** experienced in any one of these three areas will create a gap and will surface sometime in adulthood in my continuing search for happiness.

I may find myself particularly concerned with feeling **safe** in my surroundings, or particularly sensitive to the **acceptance** of others, or I may experience in myself a drive to make sure that I am **in control** of many departments in my life.

I may be afraid to take the **risk** of doing something I have never done before; I may so fear **failure** that I hold back from using abilities that others recognise I have; in my preoccupation with **control** in my life, I may impose control on my children or office staff that is not respectful of them.

I may find myself more uncomfortable than is reasonable with **insecurity**, or more vulnerable than is warranted to a measure of **disapproval**, or more upset than makes good sense when I meet with the inevitable experience of being a creature and, therefore, **not in control** of every dimension of my life.

Growth in prayer entails the **risk** of entering places I have never been before. Growth in prayer will not be possible if I am not willing to listen to the authority of my own **experience**, but want to be guided only by what others prescribe. I will not grow in deep relationship with the Lord if I am not willing to **let go** of control in prayer.

When the Lord moves closer in prayer, as he does in the Prayer of Faith, he draws the pray-er into an attitude that accepts that **some insecurity** is alright when the Lord is close, that the **approval** that really matters is the approval and acceptance of the Lord, and that surrender to the Lord in love is surrender into the Lord's **loving control** of one's person and life.

The Lord's closeness in the Prayer of Faith is allowing issues to surface from the **unconscious**. In this kind of prayer, one no longer has the control one had when one was able to pray using the imagination or words or ideas. One is vulnerable in this prayer. This vulnerability is appropriate, for one is safe in the closeness of this special Friend. But this Friend is bent on bringing me forward to become the kind of person I am made to be. Someone said of the Lord that "He loves you **as** you are, but too much to **leave** you as you are."

The Lord's healing light shines upon all the warps and shadows in one's personal make-up, that were there already but are now being revealed to oneself, because, in this new experience of prayer, one is able to let the Lord come closer and to let more love come in. What surfaces does not come up all at once, but at a pace that the Divine Therapist wants, so as to bring healing and integration into one's psyche. This Lord is one who loves, so the suffering here is only what is necessary for uncovering what needs to be healed. Suffering seems to be inevitable here. The Lord can, of course, heal even what we are not conscious of, for God touches us at all levels, but I can respond more directly at those places I am more aware of in my prayer. I may not like what I see of myself, but what surfaces for me is my genuine self at this moment, and it is where Jesus, as healer, wants to meet me with his invisible touch.

What am I to do? I am to let myself see and **feel** what is painful for me: I need to be **present** to what the Lord allows to come to the surface in me, so that I may acknowledge it as part of me at this moment, and learn from it. To quote Marcel Proust: "We are healed of a suffering only by experiencing it to the full."[20] I must not run from the pain, for this is what I have done already in the past when I did not deal with the issue when it came up first for me, for maybe I was not able to handle it then, but now I have the **opportunity** given to me. I must **stay** in the wound. There is a **gift** here for me.

What do I learn? I learn that **some** pain is all right for me to have: some insecurity, some disapproval, some lack of power. Insecurity and disapproval and want of power now **turn** me to the Lord as to the one who **fills** the painful space in me with his loving presence, his loving acceptance, his loving care. I am gradually being led to say to the Lord, "You are enough."

To quote Thomas Keating, "Happiness is intimacy with God, the experience of God's loving presence. Without that experience, nothing else quite works; with it, almost anything works."[21]

Examples
Take a person who may be particularly vulnerable to another's **impatience**:

"I can't bear it when so-and-so is impatient with me

and treats me impersonally as if I were a thing, not a person." The **disproportion** here may have come as a residue from times when Dad (or Mam) was sharp and impatient with the person in early childhood. How did one deal with it **then**? "I developed a fear of displeasing my Dad and felt **unsafe** and learnt to conform to what I thought he wanted of me."

What am I learning **now**? My Dad (or my Mam) is still inside me, limiting me. I can recognise patterns of this in how I look upon those in authority over me, and even in my attitude of fear of displeasing God. But I am ready now to unlearn this. How? By turning to God to find my safety there. I have lost my fear of displeasing God for I have already, in prayer, met the God who loves me and is intimate with me. There I am safe. I can do the same about my fear of people who are impatient with me. I need not continue to squash myself or diminish myself.

Take a person who has a heightened concern for **approval**: I often feel unsure. I am afraid of drawing criticism on myself. I keep checking out with friends what I am to do. Recently, a relative of mine was dismissive of me, and I felt so hurt. The same person's encouragement in the past gave me a great boost. I didn't expect what he said. I am aware that what he said and how he said it have come out of the pain of his own recent bereavement. I can see the **disproportion** in my reaction. I think that this sensitivity has come from my being the eldest in my family, wary of my mother's criticism.

What am I learning **now**? In prayer, I know the Lord's favour. I see that it is time for me to allow this pain of rejection without turning in upon myself and becoming self-rejecting. I will turn to the Lord. The Lord accepts me. I want him to be enough.

Take a person with issues around **control**:

> I like to know where I stand. Uncertainty makes me uneasy. I like to be certain that the person who has arranged to meet me will turn up. I am lucky to have a job at the moment, but I am not sure I will have it next year, with all the uncertainty in the job market. When I have a talk to give, I worry a lot about doing it well. Fear of failure scares me. I tend to imagine the worst possible scenario. What will happen?
>
> What am I learning **now**? When I bring my fear of failure to the Lord in prayer, I feel invited to entrust the future to him. I am like my mother: she kept worrying about things. My Dad was the opposite — laid-back, and taking each day as it came. I want to live in the present moment. When I take that attitude, I seem to feel close to the Lord. Prayer has changed to something that feels like failure, but I am becoming able to accept it. I trust it.

The Lord is the answer to my **imbalance**.

1. **Close** to him, I am safe, unafraid.
2. **Valued** by him, I am loved for who I am.
3. **Surrendered** into his loving control, I am where I belong.

It is relationship with **Jesus, the Risen Lord**, which rights my imbalance.

Chapter 6

The Cloud

"And when the priests came out of the holy place, a cloud filled the house of the Lord, so that the priests could not stand to minister because of the cloud; for the glory of the Lord filled the house of the Lord. Then Solomon said, 'The Lord has said that he would dwell in thick darkness. I have built you an exalted house, a place for you to dwell in forever.'"

(*1 Kings* 8:10-13) (NRSV)

In the last chapter, we saw that the **dark** experience Moses was given in his encounter with the Lord was **intimate communion**. It was also an experience of God's **presence**.

Our pray-er, who has been brought into the Prayer of Faith, is experiencing a dark prayer, which is **intimate communion**, for the Lord has come closer. It is also an experience of God's **presence**, though it will take time for this to be perceived.

I am learning to accept the "upstairs" activity of my imagination when I set myself to be present to my Lord. "Distractions", so called, being involuntary, are becoming less of a problem. I am coming to say "yes" to this "upstairs noise" that **accompanies** my presence to the Lord in prayer. I say "yes" now to whatever the Lord is giving me. Prayer is a time of waiting on the Lord, and staying the time.

The growing intensity of the unfelt desire for God in prayer and in life has the effect of revealing where, in my life, I am at odds with God. The Prayer of Faith is allowing a **new light** to shine in on my consciousness. My shadow-side has come into view. It feels an unwelcome sight. God, in his love, is offering **healing** in this prayer for my lack of love.

The healing rays of God's light expose deeper wounds that surface from my unconsciousness around my over-concern for security, my over-sensitivity to disapproval, and my fear of powerlessness. I recognise that my past is surfacing when I see a **disproportion** in my reaction to what has actually happened in the present. Through prayer, I grow to know that I am **safe** in the Lord's closeness, that I am **valued** by the Lord himself for who I am, and accepted by him, and that **surrender** to his power over me is where I am most at home.

The Cloud

King Solomon had spent seven years building the house of the Lord (IK 6:38) (NRSV). The interior was elaborate and extraordinarily beautiful, for no expense had been spared. And now the ark that contained the two tablets of stone placed there by Moses at Horeb had been installed by the priests in the innermost sanctuary of the house, in the most holy place (IK 8:6, 9). These two tablets symbolised the Lord's commitment to his own people and their committed response.

> "When the priests came out of the holy place, a **cloud** filled the house of the Lord ... for the **glory** of the Lord filled the house of the Lord."
> (IK 8:10-11)

Solomon recognised that God's presence or glory had come to this house under the symbol of this dark cloud:

> "Then Solomon said, 'The Lord has said that he would dwell in **thick darkness**.'"
> (IK 8:12)

The **cloud** is an apt symbol for God's presence. A cloud is mysterious and without definite shape. It is obscure; sometimes it is thick darkness. It creates a feeling of being surrounded by what has come very close. One feels lost and out of control. One can only surrender to mystery and adore.

The **cloud** is an apt metaphor for the way the Lord is present in the **Prayer of Faith**. There are no clear ideas. There is a presence that is obscure. One feels that one has lost one's way and lost control. One doesn't know where to focus, for it is like being in a cinema but one does not know where the screen is. There are no clear markers by which to measure one's situation or way.

Solomon knows that this beautiful house he has built for the Lord cannot **contain** the Lord, or localise the Lord. In the prayer he made in the presence of all the people after the cloud had filled the house, he said,

> "...But will God indeed dwell on the earth? Even heaven and the highest heaven cannot **contain** you, much less this house that I have built!" (1K 8:27) (NRSV)

He is aware of the mystery that God is. Nevertheless, Solomon is also aware that people, being creatures, need a place dedicated to God's presence. He says that people will pray **toward** this place, and that **in heaven** their prayers will be heard:

> "Hear the plea of your servant and of your people Israel when they pray **toward** this place; O hear **in heaven** your dwelling place; heed and forgive." (1K 8:30) (NRSV)

The sacred place has a special significance for the people's relationship with the Lord, but God is greater than any place. God cannot be contained in any place, yet God can make his **presence** known and felt in a place or in a person. This is mysterious. We, too, can feel the God of the Universe **present** to us or in us in prayer. We can feel the Risen Jesus **present** to us or in us in prayer. In the Prayer of Faith, there is a gradual awareness that the darkness is holding a presence.

The Experience

Our praying person is being faithful to giving regular time in prayer and is finding it easier now to **accept** how prayer is for her. These accounts below indicate how the experience is developing:

> It took me a good while before I noticed something other than the shifting images on the surface or my sense of frustration with the dryness. It was like being in a room where the lights had been turned off and you could see nothing. Gradually, you would

begin to notice a **candle** there with its soft, flickering flame, and be surprised at how much became visible, though without any clear outline. What I 'saw', as it were, was a sense of my attention being held, and a sense of Someone present, but I couldn't look at this directly. The experience resembled **'peripheral vision'**: you know you are aware of something at the edge, but it eludes **direct focus.**

Another comparison came to me, that of hearing a sound at the edge of hearing. I was aware of holding myself very still, as if I was trying to pick up **a very distant sound.** This prayer experience seems to be a non-event, yet I very much want to be there. I am beginning to notice something. There's something paradoxical about it.

I am becoming used to the **two levels** in my prayer. Last autumn, I was leaning on a small bridge over a little stream. I was gazing at the water and began to notice how **clear** it was. Some leaves came by, floating on the surface, and then a twig, and then more small leaves, but I didn't follow any of them with my eye. I kept my gaze on the **lovely clarity** of the water. Something like that is happening now in my prayer. I let the two levels **co-exist**, and am more aware of the deeper level. I am more aware of my experience of **myself** and how **peaceful** I can be at times. Something is **holding** me.

The Cloud as Presence

The mixed experience that is Prayer of Faith gradually begins to reveal itself as **presence.**

I remember Fr Paul Kennedy SJ, saying in my presence, "The great thing is to **want** the darkness. The darkness is his **presence.**" People find this to be a very helpful saying. Our pray-er is growing in unselfishness through being in prayer on God's terms, and is consistent in turning up to give herself to the Lord in this kind of prayer. This generosity enables the person to become at ease with the experience of it, and also to become sensitive to what is being given there. By **wanting** the "upstairs" level to be there, one becomes able to perceive, in the "downstairs" level, the Lord's presence. One notices that something is happening, that something is being given. One feels engaged with; one feels calmed and held; one feels a peace. It is an experience registering in one's body. One is now able to notice this because one is welcoming the whole experience, however it is. Faith is able to interpret this as the effect of God's secret action. Darkness now feels more like **obscurity**, for there is some kind of light perceived there.

One is now appreciating the truth of what the author of *The Cloud of Unknowing* says:

> Thought cannot comprehend God. And so, I prefer to abandon all I can know, choosing rather to **love** him whom I cannot know. Though we cannot know him we can love him. **By love he may be touched and embraced, never by thought.**[22]

Whom does one meet in the Cloud?
Who is present there?

For **Solomon** and his fellow Israelites, the one present in the Cloud was the Lord, the Creator, the Deliverer, the One who had chosen Israel as his "treasured possession". (*Deut* 7:6)

> The Lord did not set his affection on you because you were more numerous than other peoples, for you were the fewest of all peoples. But it was because the Lord **loved** you ...that he brought you out with a mighty hand and redeemed you from the land of slavery, from the power of Pharaoh king of Egypt. Know therefore that the Lord your God **is** God; he is the faithful God... (*Deut* 7:7-9) (NIV)

For **Solomon** and the people of Israel, the Lord was the one who had chosen to enter into their life; the initiative was his. He had done this because of love, **an unearned love**. He had chosen to be involved. The 'thick darkness' of the cloud could not be represented by any image or idol. The Cloud was an awesome presence in the most holy place in the house of the Lord. God is mysterious and yet intimately close; awesome but loving; loving, and awaiting a response. The response was to be worship and obedience.

For the **baptised Christian**, the one present in the Cloud is the Father of Jesus. In *Matthew* 6:6, Jesus tells me that "my Father" is waiting for me when I enter prayer, waiting for me "in secret", that is, out of sight, beyond the reach of my senses. Can I see my Father? Yes, and no.

In the earlier stages of prayer, and for a long time, Jesus himself was the image of the Father that I was seeing, for Jesus is the full expression, in human terms, of the Father. Then, as Jesus drew closer and took over my prayer, images even of Jesus stopped being of help during prayer. My prayer became imageless because it was going deeper, and Jesus was leading me to a share in his own prayer where there is no image. He led me to the Father.

And what was waiting for me? I met this Mysterious One, who is the Godhead, the Source of all there is, whom Jesus reveals as loving, tender, caring and welcoming, and as utterly desirable, and as encompassing all the qualities of a mother and a father. This is the one who is present in the Cloud that is the Prayer of Faith. Jesus has led me to a further participation in his own prayer of communion with his Father.

The response
This is my Father; this is the Father of Jesus. **My response**, like that of Solomon, and like that of Jesus, must be one of adoration, awe, before sheer mystery. And like Jesus, too, I **receive** from my Father a share in the utter love that Jesus is receiving from his Father.

This Cloud is a special 'place'. The loss of the old forms of prayer that had been so helpful is replaced by what is so beautiful an enrichment. It is only **faith** that enables me to **see** into this dark cloud and be grateful for the gift of the Father's new closeness to me.

Listen to Him

When Peter, John and James were on the Mount of Transfiguration with Jesus, they had an experience of the cloud. It was the Father coming close to them and revealing himself.

> A cloud appeared and enveloped them, and they
> were afraid as they entered the cloud. A voice came
> from the cloud, saying, 'This is my Son, whom I
> have chosen; listen to him.' (*Luke* 9:34-35)

The cloud surrounded them and they felt afraid: an unaccustomed closeness does cause fear. It was the nearness of the Father. "They entered the cloud," we are told. It was the Father's **embrace** they entered, for this cloud was carrying and concealing his loving presence. This was their share, you might say, of what had happened for Jesus in his encounter with his Father on the mountain. The Father was coming as close to them as they could take. Notice that he revealed himself by focusing their attention on his Son: "This is my Son...**listen to him.**"

The Father, from the cloud of the Prayer of Faith, points us back to his Son. This is what he wants for us. We are to listen to everything we learn about Jesus. We are to keep returning to his teaching and to his example. As the author of the *Letter to the Hebrews* puts it, "**Let us fix our eyes on Jesus**, the author and perfecter of our faith." (*Heb* 12:2)

Spiritual Reading

This raises the topic of spiritual reading. We are no longer able to focus our full attention on Jesus' message during our time of prayer, but we can continue to let ourselves be formed by Jesus **outside** of prayer by active reflection on what is revealed in scripture.

In this prayer we know Jesus **directly**; in our reflection on scripture, we know **about** Jesus. Both kinds of knowing are necessary for us, for this is how we are made. To give breadth and depth to what we know in our **direct** awareness, we are to feed on the revelation already given to us in the scriptures. Our dark prayer has the advantage of making us more perceptive to what we read and reflect on in the scriptures. There is an **invisible light** shining into our consciousness during the Prayer of Faith – it is invisible, like white light – and so, when we come to give our attention to God's scriptural word afterwards, the text lights up and we discover insights. In this kind of reading we grow in our knowledge of the One who, in our experience of full prayer, is hidden. The first reason for spiritual reading, then, is out of obedience to the Father's direction to us: "*Listen to him*".

Spiritual reading becomes significant also for a **second** reason. By "spiritual" I do not mean just any spiritual book; I mean the reading in which this person is finding **relish now**, not instruction or information, but delight, savour. I say relish **now**, for the book that gave relish once may not appeal to the heart a year later. This is especially true when Prayer of Faith has taken hold. Because prayer has now become **inarticulate**, (beyond the use of words or images), the emotions and the fantasy can have no direct part in it. But the emotions and the fantasy are yearning for some participation in the person's involvement with the hidden, unimaginable God; and it is in spiritual reading that he can find this, and indeed he **needs** to have it. The spiritual reading in which one finds relish gives articulation to a relationship, which, in prayer, is inarticulate; in the reading, we hear what we already know but is hidden. Through this kind of reading, the levels of the self that are being by-passed by God's action get involved and are satisfied, and so the whole self is drawn into God's attracting. The dryness of Prayer of Faith becomes easier to bear.

Underground Stream: Prayer & Daily Life

People who pray like this come to recognise that, although **during** the time of prayer nothing much seemed to be going on, apart from the superficial flow of random fantasies, they are certain, during the rest of the day, that something was received which is empowering them to cope with their situation and to be patient, to be spontaneously unselfish and to be able to let go of their plans when an unexpected request intrudes: there is surrender of self **in** prayer and **in** life. Prayer is like an **underground stream,** which breaks the surface only later during the day. Or to take another person's image, the effect of the dark prayer in daily life is like bulbs now sprouting above ground. Faith is now able to say "yes", during prayer, to the gift that is, as yet, hidden, and then to recognise it afterwards during the day as from God in whatever shape it materialised. For God is empowering the person during prayer; the person knows it afterwards. This dark prayer is, indeed, precious. There is an exchange of love here: love received and love given. The Lord is close. To quote the author of *The Cloud of Unknowing,* "By **love** he may be touched and embraced, never by thought."[23] Love is developing. The love I give is a love already received.

A Benign Darkness
Prayer continues to be a 'benign darkness', a sense of inner poverty, a sense of at-home-ness with mystery. There can be a harmony or uneventfulness in such prayer. It resembles the experience of putting one's hand into water of the same temperature as one's hand, without looking. You do not know whether your hand is in it or not. This harmony is a good sign.

Nothing much can be reported about such a prayer-experience, except that there is a certain **variation** in it, some life, and eventually a varying intensity, a sense that the imagination is sometimes more stilled, and this not by one's own doing: there may be a degree of absorption.

The conversation with the spiritual director at this stage is likely to centre much more on life outside of prayer: the attempt to surrender to God's will in one's circumstances in life.

Chapter 7
Union

"He must increase, but I must decrease."
(*John* 3:30) (NRSV)

In the last chapter, we reflected on the story of King Solomon and how the **presence**, or **glory**, of the Lord filled the house of the Lord with **a cloud of thick darkness**. Solomon, however, realised at the same time that no place can **contain** the Lord. He was aware of the mystery that God is. Yet, the God of the Universe can be present to us, and in us, in prayer. The darkness of the Prayer of Faith is holding **a presence**. One must **want** this darkness. One then, gradually, becomes aware of an experience of feeling acted upon, that something is **given**.

For the **baptised Christian**, the one present in the Cloud is the **Father** of Jesus. Faith enables me to see into this dark cloud as the Father's presence to me; and He is **pointing** me to Jesus and saying: **"Listen to him."** This dark prayer is like an **underground stream** breaking the surface later during the day. The focus of the person's growth shifts to life **outside** of prayer, namely, to grow in surrender to God's will in one's circumstances in life.

I noted that we can continue to let ourselves be formed by Jesus **outside** of prayer by our active reflection on scripture and by spiritual reading.

And now let us approach this new chapter.

A Wedding is Intimated

John the Baptist saw that he must **make room** for Jesus. The time had come. John was told by some of his disciples:

> Rabbi, that man who was with you on the other side of the Jordan – the one you testified about – well, he is baptising, and **everyone** is going to him. (*John* 3:26) (NIV)

This was good news for John. John knew his place. His active ministry must **make way** for another's activity – that of Jesus. *"He must increase, but I must decrease."* His own **activity** must wane and allow the **activity** of Jesus to move onto centre stage.

John speaks of a bridegroom and a bride: "The bride belongs to the bridegroom." (NIV) **A wedding is intimated.** The wedding of humanity to the divinity has already happened, in essence, in the incarnation of the Son of God. **Jesus is the wedding**, you could say. And now Jesus is at work offering to bring us, one by one, into a conscious share in this marriage. How? By drawing us into **union with himself**, so as to have a share with him of what he has – his union with the Father. We are **called** to become wedded to God by receiving a share in the sonship of Jesus: to be sons and daughters by adoption. We are **called** to a share in the **Spirit** of Jesus, who is the bond of love between Father and Son in the Trinity. We are **called** into a love relationship. We are **called** to be led by love, led by the same Spirit as Jesus was.

Open to all Christians

This calling has begun already. In our baptism, we are given the **seed** of this vocation. Our journey of prayer is the development of what has started in us at our baptism. The Prayer of Faith and its flowering in contemplation is open to all Christians. To quote Thomas Keating, "The genuine Christian tradition, taught uninterruptedly for the first fifteen centuries, is that contemplation is the normal evolution of a genuine spiritual life and hence is **open to all Christians.**"[24]

"I must decrease."

As I have already said, John the Baptist's activity in ministry must **wane** and allow the activity of Jesus in ministry to move onto centre stage. Something similar has already been happening for the person of Prayer of Faith. Activity in prayer by use of mental focus and effort has been **waning** in order to allow Jesus to be the active one, more and more, by the "secret inflow of loving wisdom" that is flowing in directly below the level of mental focus and effort.

Jesus is moving closer and taking more part in the person's prayer and in the person's daily life and desires. "For God so loved the world that he **gave** his only Son, so that everyone who **believes** in him may not perish but may have **eternal** life." (*John* 3:16) (NRSV) God not only sent his Son but also **gave** his Son. We are to **have** him by our **faith** relationship with him. By faith I enter into the **circle** of friendship with Jesus. Faith means belonging, intimate connection. This belonging is "eternal life"; what is here now will last forever. This is what is developing in the Prayer of Faith. There is a growing closeness. And because Jesus is also the Holy One, closeness to him in prayer and life reveals not only his extraordinary love for me, but also the areas in my life that reveal my want of love. So, a further **purification** continues as the closeness grows.

A Shift in Consciousness

The person experiencing the Prayer of Faith is becoming accustomed to accepting the two levels in the experience of prayer, namely, the upstairs disarray and the downstairs desire for God. Because he has stopped feeling at odds with the upstairs flotsam and jetsam, he is beginning to notice that there is more going on downstairs where he is present to his desire for the Lord. He is saying, as it were, "Here I am Lord: I am here to do your will." (cf. *Heb* 10:7; *Psalm* 40:7-8) He is noticing how he is affected in his experience. He notes a certain peace, a peace that has a subtle variation in it; it is quietly alive. His desire, too, has a certain life in it: the thought, "I have come to do your will" brings on a passing surge of desire to surrender. Of course, he can't hold on to the thought, but it puts words on how he is at that moment. The dryness, too, is varying, being sometimes painful. Here, awareness in prayer has moved to his state of consciousness.

The shift **from** mental focus **to** attention to experience now becomes more pronounced. For years, his prayer was with the ideas, images and words that carried his communication with the Lord. This changed when the Prayer of Faith came on, and mental effort no longer connected him in prayer: only attitude and desire could help him in prayer. But, at the same time, his imagination was still at work in an unhelpful way while he sought the Lord in desire for him. But now, at last, he is no longer anxious about the involuntary distractions and can accept them and, in fact, **wants** them to be part of his presence to the Lord, for this is the prayer that the Lord is giving to him. The result is that his awareness is changing **from** the level of the 'distractions' **to** the level of his state of **consciousness**: he is able to pick up what is happening inside him. There is more peace in him to do this because he is more attuned to God's will in his daily life.

Experience and Union with God

People vary in regard to experience. The **introverted** person is more self-aware and quicker to notice her inner state and to find words to describe it. An **extraverted** person, being less inward-looking, finds it harder to notice the variation in his inner state, and is less interested in it, preferring to be engaged with what is outside. God deals with us as we are and uses our strengths for his own purposes. Union with God is **essentially** at the level of our **will**. Our psychological awareness does not measure this. So, one person may be very much aware in prayer of how her inner state is, and another be unable to notice much of what is going on inside himself, and yet their union with God's will, their surrender to God, their holiness, could be equal. Experience, and awareness of it, is not the measure of where our heart is.

Going Deeper

Given that we are not speaking of degrees of holiness, we may speak of the **experience** of prayer going deeper. A person may experience another transition in prayer, a shift into an ease with this kind of praying, a sense that surrender into it has been given: it is called Prayer of Union.

Here is one person's experience.

Prayer had put down roots in my life during the previous two years. I was in love with this man. My love for him had touched into a depth in myself much more than I realised. Dryness in prayer came with the breakdown of this relationship. Before this, words and images held me in prayer; I was able to encounter Jesus through a scripture passage, and even a word or phrase was becoming enough for prolonged attention on the Lord. I could lean on phrases such as, 'The Lord is my shepherd.' I could imagine Jesus walking beside me and asking me, 'What are you carrying in your heart today?' And then, with the breakdown of my love relationship, the dryness came. I couldn't pray. I could only be there. I felt quite unable to pray. This inability lasted for three months and was very painful. As my former way of praying no longer connected me with the Lord, I took a break from the Retreat in Daily Life (*The Spiritual Exercises* of St Ignatius), while I stayed in the dryness and negotiated my feelings around the pain of loss.

Then something happened. One day, I happened to be watching a movie that carried a line about God being present in the eyes of a dying, homeless woman. The young man said to his friend, 'When I looked into her eyes, it seemed as though God looked back at me in that moment.' This opened a chink into my own heart. It was an experiential knowing, something I could not doubt. I began to see that God could be present, and, indeed, **was** present, in my own experience of loss and pain. It gave me something to hold on to. From then on, I began to sense that I was meeting God in a deeper part of myself. Something else I knew in that moment was that God's love was not something earned but is a free gift, and is constant, whatever way I would be feeling in myself. This was deeply consoling. In the weeks that followed, I began to experience God's consolation as something delicate and quiet and barely perceptible. This awareness of God's presence grew. I was in a deeper place in myself; and I was meeting Jesus there. This developed.

I began to get over the experience of loss. I resumed the Retreat in Daily Life: prayer now was quiet, so, outside of prayer, I reflected on texts about the life of Christ that my director gave me.

One night, about three years later, I sat down to pray. During my prayer, I had this experience. Every part of me felt drawn to the centre of myself. I felt taken over. There were no thoughts or feelings or emotions: just darkness enveloping me. I was out of my depth in this unknown place. No words seemed adequate to describe what was happening. It was just darkness. I had the impression that I was going into a deep sleep, but yet I was awake and aware. My mouth became dry, and I felt a touch of nausea for a while. I knew that something had been done to me, but, afterwards, I had a feeling of peace and strength.

After this, my desire for prayer grew. Prayer felt easier. There was a clear sense of receiving in prayer. I felt I was being nourished.

Outside of prayer, I became less self-focused. I became more considerate with others, particularly with members of my own family. I was aware of a new gentleness in myself; I noticed this particularly when driving my car. I became more flexible towards my work-colleagues. It became easier for me to be in the present moment. I noticed, too, that the prayer allayed some of my anxieties.

Another person experienced this transition differently:

I remember the moment when prayer changed. I had been consistent in giving myself to God in the bare experience over a period of about nine years. I wanted to be there for his sake, even if I was drawing no delight or satisfaction. My attitude was that God deserved my time. Then one day, before the midday meal, I knelt in my room for a quarter of an hour's prayer, and after five minutes I felt myself taken over. It was like being possessed for a few minutes. I was filled with a sense of presence. It was a warm experience. I had not known about this. I wasn't frightened. I went with it. I felt happy.

What struck me most was the effect it had on me **outside** of prayer. There was a member of staff who many of us found unpleasant to deal with, but this time I found myself warm-hearted and accepting towards him. This surprised me. I knew that the change in me was coming from what had just happened for me, the new closeness in prayer.

Each time I sat for prayer after that, I had a strong sense that this prayer was being given. I had only to receive. I began to read Chapman's *Spiritual Letters* and found them a great help.

Negotiating this new experience

Let us describe what the experience might be.

I approach this time of Prayer of Faith as I usually do.

I begin by connecting with myself: 'How am I?' I pause. I slow down. I remind myself that this prayer time is a meeting: Someone is waiting for me. When I feel ready, I raise my focus off myself: I look towards the Lord. He is looking at me. I don't see him, but, in faith, I know he is here. 'How is he looking at me?' He is looking at me with love and desire. I want to rest here under his loving gaze. How am I to negotiate this time of prayer? I ask to be shown. I want to be led. I want to be here more for him than for myself. I ask his grace for this. Whatever experience of prayer I am given, that is what I want, or, at least, that is what I want to want.

Then I wait. I must wait for the Lord's initiative. I don't try to control my surface awareness: I let it shift. If some thought or concern begins to capture my focus, I draw back gently in some way, and let my focus move down towards the interior darkness. I feel a bit helpless. It is like walking on a tightrope. I want to become less aware of myself, for I know that this disposes me for being caught off my guard by the Lord. (It is like a time when I was on the shore watching the waves flowing in, one after the other. Each new wave was like the one before it, but yet slightly different. So, I couldn't study them. Then I found my attention becoming splayed out.)

Here, now, I am less aware of myself, and before I realise it, something has changed. I am caught off guard. I am receiving something. It is like catching a whiff of an exquisite **perfume**. I draw it in. My attention is arrested. In this moment, I feel enchanted. It is his presence, the presence of the Risen Lord. I am calm. I feel held. Some gentle power is acting upon me, and my body picks this up. I sense the Lord is close. My attention has shifted from my thoughts and images to this new attraction. I am held by this. I want to hold on to it. I float for a while. Then the feeling is gone. It has **slipped** from my grasp. What remains is a certain peace. This peace is also his presence.

Perfume

The metaphor of perfume conveys well the experience of the Lord's presence. Perfume suggests very strongly the powerful attraction of the Lord in prayer. *"Delicate is the fragrance of your perfume,"* we read in the *Song of Songs* 1:2 (JB). Blaise Arminjon SJ says in his commentary on those words:

> What enchants her is his **perfume**, this perfume that follows him everywhere and radiates from him: this perfume that **announces** his arrival and also lingers for a long time after him; this perfume that is uniquely his, absolutely unique in the world, that is immaterially his very presence, and that causes his Bride, when she inhales it, to say immediately and without hesitation: there he is, **this is he!**[25]

When Jesus addressed Mary Magdalen by name in the garden (*John* 20), she was caught off guard. She wasn't expecting this. Here was someone who knew her. When she recognised who it was, she felt overwhelmed, arrested in wonder. She wanted to hold him, and not only to hold him but **also** to hold on to him. But he had a **deeper** presence in store for her. Meantime, she was to learn how to **let go** and yet to **have**.

The person experiencing the Prayer of Faith, wants, like Mary, to cling to the presence given to him. This presence is so good, so attractive, and so personal. But the Lord has a **deeper** gift to give to him. So, he has yet to learn by painful experience that the **experience** of closeness is one thing, and the **closeness** itself is another. In the **experience**, he hears the Lord say, among other things, "I am here." But experience cannot be permanent; it is a passing movement; it must change. It is the **message** of the experience that remains: "I am here and I love you, always." It is this that the Lord wants him to take possession of. He is tempted to try to **prolong** the experience instead of letting it flow. So he has to learn to welcome, and yet **let go** of, the experiences that are given to him in prayer, and to **cling,** instead, to the message of the Lord's abiding presence, whether felt or not felt.

A story may help. This couple are in a mature relationship. On Sunday, he tells his wife, "I love you so much." She is enchanted and full of gratitude. On Monday, he doesn't say it, nor on Tuesday, nor on any other day of that week. She notes this. She is living on the memory of what he said on Sunday. It would please her very much to hear him say his love again, but she resists any desire to steer him round to saying it. She is sure of his abiding love, anyway, and **trusts** this. But, on the next Sunday, he says to her, "Oh, if only I could tell you how much I love you!" This time his word of love is even more delightful to her, she having fasted, as it were, from expressions of love for many days. She was free enough to do without, and now she hears his love with enhanced delight, knowing he has not been forced by any hint from her. It is his free gift.

God deals like this with us. He weans us from **self-interest** in prayer. He draws us to grow in **trust** that he can only love us. Trust is an issue of growing importance in our relationship with the Lord.

Faith Interprets Experience

People speak of their experience in prayer in terms of what they feel. "I felt held" is a frequent description. "I felt loved"; "I felt the Lord was close to me"; "I felt great peace arise in me"; "I felt my anxiety change to a confidence that all would be well: I felt calm".

Faith sees into the meaning of what is happening in the prayer, namely, that this experience, picked up in her sense of touch, is the Lord's presence. This is an interpretation of the experience, a faith interpretation. Touch is the primary sense, and is the one most apt for registering what is happening.

It is an interpretation, I say, for the sense of touch itself cannot **directly** perceive God, for God is spirit. Touch can **directly** perceive only what is physical, like itself, such as, an apple. I can touch an apple, see it, taste it, smell it, and hear the crunch it makes when I bite on it.

But I am composed of soul and body, or spirit and sense. So I can **indirectly** perceive God's active presence in my prayer through my sense of touch. For when God, in the Prayer of Faith, is bypassing my sense level so as to act directly on my spirit level, I can know that God is doing something by the way my body is **reacting** in prayer. What I experience **directly** is myself reacting in my feeling of touch, but by faith I can **interpret** this feeling as God's active presence upon me. My **direct** experience is of myself: my experience of God, then, is **indirect**.

The sense of touch

Now, God can indeed act on me in my spiritual level **without** any echo happening in my bodily level, and does so. But God regularly chooses to cause my body to react to His inflow, and I am saying that this is commonly picked up by me in my sense of touch. For touch, I say, is the primary sense, and is the one most apt for registering **indirectly** God's **direct** active presence in my soul during prayer. By faith I interpret this experience and learn something of God's meaning. The extent of my bodily reaction will depend on my temperament.

When a baby is born, the sense through which she or he is affirmed is the sense of touch. The baby's whole skin surface is available for the message of care and love through the touch, which says, "I want you". To be held and caressed is essential for the baby to know what is being communicated by the mother. Primal messages are received through the sense of touch.

Is it any wonder, then, that touch is also, for the adult, the medium of intimacy? Where a friendship is deep and true, to be touched or held or caressed or kissed is the language of intimate presence and love. Words are not enough; seeing is not enough; it is the sense of touch that conveys the experience of deep closeness. God uses this dimension of our makeup to let us know that he is close and loving.

Touch is a diffuse, pervasive sense, just as the cloud that symbolised God's presence in Solomon's Temple (1K 8), that I referred to in the previous chapter, is diffuse, pervasive, undefined, and of indefinite shape. When there is cloud, we can't see: we grope our way forward; we try to feel our way, for we are blindfolded, as it were. In the Prayer of Faith we are, also, as though blindfolded, unable to see, and it is the experience of touch that lets us know of God's loving presence. Darkness becomes luminous through the sense of touch and through faith.

Two Freedoms Meet

In this experience of prayer, two freedoms meet: **divine** freedom and **human** freedom.

God, for His part, is always pouring in His love, the love that gives me existence; he gives me being, as he gives being to every creature. But he is also offering me **relationship**. In the meeting that is prayer, he is **choosing** when to let me know his presence and action. He is choosing when to reveal his active presence, which I pick up in my sense of touch. This **varies** because God wants me not to become more attached to the **sign** of his presence than to **himself**: I am to love and want the **Giver** rather than the **gift**. I welcome the gift, but I must learn that the Giver is present even when not perceived by me. My experience of this variation teaches me that I cannot **command** this feeling of his presence. From this I learn that when I do pick up, in my sense of touch, that the Lord is lovingly present to me, I have not produced this myself, and so I can **trust** that what I perceive is truly from God. I am in a real relationship.

There is also freedom on my part, but I misuse it at times. I know that I ought to be in prayer on God's terms, but my **self-interest** intrudes at times: this narrows down my openness in prayer. I know that it is God's will that I should desire, but my **self-will** raises its head and I want to do my own thing instead. I know that God is drawing me to making him be king of my heart, but my **self-love** sometimes does not want the pain of letting go of some attachment where I find security, and this restricts God's access to my experience.

Balance

There is yet another way in which I could place myself **beyond** picking-up God's consolation in prayer. When I become over-eager for some project I have taken on, even for God, and push myself hard and drive my body, I can become unable to sense God's active presence in my sense of touch. I am treating my body hard. I am driven. I have lost the **balance** between soul and body that is right for me. I am ignoring my body's need. I am not respecting my body. I am not listening to what God is saying to me through my body's need.

St Ignatius, in the First Week of the *Spiritual Exercises*, speaks of this balance between soul and body and the role this plays in receiving consolation, when he speaks of the role of penance. In this part of the Exercises, Ignatius invites the exercitant to ask for various graces, such as, embarrassment at his/her sins, sorrow for them, and felt knowledge of them and so on. He expects these graces to register in felt consolation. In #89, he says:

> When someone fails to find what he or she desires, such as tears, consolation, and the like, it is often useful to make some **change** in eating, sleeping, and other forms of penance, so that we do penance for two or three days, and then omit it for two or three days. Furthermore, for some persons more penance is suitable, and, for others, less.

He goes on to say that on many occasions we give up penance because we indulge ourselves and think erroneously that the penance would make us ill. On the other hand, we sometimes do excessive penance, thinking that the body can bear it. Then Ignatius, speaking from wisdom born of experience, says,

> Now since God our Lord knows our nature infinitely better than we do, through changes of this sort he often enables us to know what is right for ourselves.[26]

What Ignatius implies here is that when we have found the right balance between our desire and our body, God's approval will register in the consoling presence he makes us feel.

The Journey

The journey of Prayer of Faith continues. It will be a long journey. A new part of the journey has now begun.

Essentially, it is about **surrender** to the Lord in love. There is surrender of self in prayer and also in life. "He must increase, but I must decrease." (*John* 3:30) The Lord's part increases, my part decreases. God is the one who is at work, and our part is to learn to cooperate. What is God doing? God is making space for himself in the prayer and daily life of the person. God is **increasing** his sway over the person who is willing to **decrease** his/her independence of will. This is a love relationship. The Lord is making his delicate presence felt **whenever he chooses**. Sometimes, it becomes an absorbing presence; sometimes, prayer seems to be only in my desire. I learn to dance with the variation, accepting that I am not in control. "If any want to become my followers, let them deny themselves..." (*Luke* 9:23) (NRSV) So, I wait on his gift. Something in me is being **displaced** by having to wait. I am learning how to cooperate. There are times when I am sure I am held; there are other times when prayer is not obvious and I ask myself, "Am I praying? Is there something wrong?" I am **anxious**. I try to contribute some effort in prayer, but it doesn't work. Then, the next day, I am floating again, entranced by the fragrance of his presence. This time, I am tempted to **prolong** this experience instead of letting it flow.

I am like a person who has a ball of mercury resting on his open palm; if I close my hand to possess it, the mercury simply runs off along a groove in my palm. In the same way, I cannot succeed in **holding on** to whatever experience of closeness I am given. To use another metaphor: it is like a butterfly that has landed somehow on my open palm; keeping my hand open, I admire its beauty; I don't know how long it will stay; I daren't take possession of it by closing my hand.

I learn to **receive**, and to **let go**. This variation in experience is hard to bear. I feel insecure. I feel like a patient on an operating table, unable to contribute. The Lord is like a surgeon needing me to receive only, to let him be fully in charge. I must trust that God is engaged with me even when I am not sure I feel this. There is **gain** in this new experience of prayer, and yet there is also some kind of **loss**, for my control is displaced. I walk on a tight-rope.

Reaching outwards

This prayer is a loving surrender, which is unable, as yet, to become full surrender. One is receiving God's action, and yet one also feels a striving, a reaching outwards to God. It is a time when, in the words of de Caussaude, "the soul lives in God," [27] and so there is that sense of reaching outwards. Though God is giving, God is also **drawing,** and the person feels stretched. God is addressing the intellect and the will directly in a powerful way. It is the Cloud, the Father, drawing closer. God is revealing himself mysteriously, and the person's desire for God is increasing. In this long stage, prayer may become intense at times, while remaining dark; the mind and the will are drawn intently, even to ecstasy or near-ecstasy, when a near total concentration and love is being drawn from the person.

Some pray-ers can know what is happening, because they are by nature more self-aware. Iain Matthew distinguishes in *The Impact of God*, between a "saint" and a "mystic". He writes,

> In turning to John, we are being approached by a saint, and a mystic. As a saint, he was greatly surrendered to the action of God. As a mystic, he experienced that action as, in some sense, manifest.[28]

A "contemplative", too, is surrendering to God's action; a "mystic" experiences that action as, in some sense, manifest. It would seem that the difference is in the awareness; some pray-ers can see better into what is going on in their experience. It is the same grace of prayer.

About Experience in Prayer

We are embodied spirits; each of us is a composite of body and spirit, and inextricably so. So, in prayer, the loving inflow of God, when it is strong or stronger than usual, tends to register in the body: the body tenses up to deal with it, somewhat like the way it reacts to cold or heat, until it becomes acclimatised to it. The **reaction** in us is not an exact measure of what we have received at the dark level of our spirit beyond the range of our senses. God touches us, not at our sense-level but in our spirit-level, but because we are embodied spirits, what has happened at the level of our spirit tends to cause a reaction that is bodily. God touches us lightly, but our reaction varies from person to person.

A story may illustrate what I mean. I remember having breakfast on the final morning of their retreat with a group of six Sisters whom I had accompanied. The phone rang. A Sister came back to say, "Mary, the call is for you." Mary, being excitable, exclaimed, "Oh!", and jumped up and hurried out to take the call. Ten minutes later, the phone rang again. This time, a Sister announced to Teresa, "The call is for you." Teresa continued talking and finished what she was saying and went out to take the call.

The message in each case was, "The call is for you". The reaction described the person, not the message.

Negotiating the experience

What registers in **experience** is not the important thing. Even **ecstasy** or near-ecstasy is not to be valued as important. Take, as a metaphor, the experience of listening to an orchestra playing the first movement of a symphony:

One listener is able to note the first violins announcing the **theme**, and then how the clarinets pick up the theme; next the second violins play the theme with a slight variation, and then the oboes render it. Next the whole orchestra is engaged. The listener enjoys observing the **structure** of this music, how the composer has assembled it. He is also moved by the music itself. He holds the two levels together, the understanding level and the feeling level.

A second listener is hearing differently. She hears the opening theme and lets it charm her; the clarinets make it sound even richer; but when the oboes play, her whole being is moved, and she feels caught up by what is **expressed** by the structure, be it a mood, or delight, or love, or beauty or wonder, thus getting in touch with what the composer was trying to express through the structure of the music. Her habitual preference is to pay attention to the experience itself, and she lets her understanding function differently, maybe feeling hereslf uplifted by delight or energy.

It is natural for us to seek to make **sense** of our experience. Our experience is comprised of feelings and meanings or thoughts. There is no "pure experience". Our experience is always a **sandwich** of two layers: a layer of feelings, and a layer of thoughts or meaning. Feelings bring thoughts; and thoughts tend to bring feelings. Thoughts come in to make **sense** of the feelings: we want to know the meaning. This is the way we are made.

So, when we experience a surge of love in prayer and have the **feeling** of being loved and caught up, we automatically grasp the **meaning** of it, namely, that we are being engaged by God here, and loved. This is because of the natural inclination in us to make sense of what is happening in us.

Intensity in prayer

Our **feeling** in prayer can become **intense** in response to God's loving inflow. This intensity becomes **tension** if we try to **hold on** to the intensity. It is as if we are too focused on the meaning and, in a way, trying to **control** the prayer. One can notice that one is trying to hold on to the intensity in order to **prolong** its presence, or trying to **add** one's effort to it in order to give more of oneself. This holding on and this effort are in the way and will bring on tension. It is in the way because the Lord wants to be the active one and wants the person just to receive, and even to be displaced. We are to allow the Lord to be fully in charge. The Lord gives and the Lord takes away. Some people are more ready to let go into **mystery**, and be carried by the love, trusting it and not wishing to control it.

Intensity in prayer may be like this. God is radiating his love and the person is captivated and feels caught up. The one who is more inclined to **make meaning** of what is happening to her will accept this nearness of God with a certain degree of **tension** until she learns to bring her mind down in some way to the darkness within, which is below meaning. There she will let go into mystery and relax and be carried beyond control. Some people are better at letting the experience happen, and their mental quest is more of **entrusting** themselves into mystery and love. Andre Louf, in his book, *Teach Us to Pray*, has this quotation from St Anthony the Hermit:

"It is not perfect prayer if the monk perceives he is praying." / *"Non est perfecta oratio in qua se monachus vel hoc ipsum quod orat intelligit."*[29] Literally, "It is not perfect prayer if the monk is aware of himself or of the fact that he is praying."[30]

I don't know if this is universally valid, but it is to be respected as a profound saying that has come down from one of the early Fathers of the Church. It points the direction forward, namely, that of being willing to let go of consciousness of self in prayer if this is where the Lord is leading and to let go into mystery. This would be by God's gift. What may seem to be loss is truly gain.

An Image in Prayer

People whose prayer is imageless speak from time to time, especially during retreat, of an image seen during prayer. It may be the image of a path leading away to a bend and out of sight, or of a boat on the sea, rudderless, or of being washed up on an island; or it may be a vision of Christ embracing oneself, or of being nailed with him. It can be a sudden flash barely glimpsed, or it can be an extended beholding. The union with Christ is going on **unseen** in the depths, and here a **symbolic image** – or it could be a word or a phrase – is thrown up from the depths to the surface consciousness.

The function of the vision is to reveal to the person what

is going on unseen in the relationship, and to give reassurance and to elicit cooperation. It functions like an image in a dream, revealing what is deeper in the psyche. I have noticed that this is particularly true of a vision of Christ: the experience going on within in the spirit can be too terrifying and awesome – he is Lord – and so the vision is needed to **reassure** the person that all is well and that the reaction experienced is the effect of Christ's closeness, in a spiritual way, to the person's spirit. The real thing is **below** words and images: the words and images are merely an **overflow** or echo of it. For we do not experience God directly: it is the self's reaction to God's deeper action that is experienced directly. Experience of God is only **indirect**.

Response

As the prayer deepens, one is more and more exposed to the God who is Love. In connection with this, and continuing with the notion of "overflow", I want to mention a kind of response that I have met with in many people. I am speaking of a prayer that is imageless and in which God is touching the person in a spiritual way, either at the level of the spiritual faculties of intellect and will, or, more usually, at a receptivity below them which is usually termed "spirit". Because we are a composite of body and soul, or of sense and spirit, and inextricably so, the love being received in the spirit can, if it is a sudden and unaccustomed infusion, be echoed in the level of sense, and, being love, it may be experienced as a delicate and intimate inner feeling. Some people read this right, and accept it; others, believing something to be wrong here, resist it. But, in fact, it is quite harmless. If one resists it, it keeps happening: it is like staying on the threshold of this place. If one accepts it, it is soon modified and eventually goes away according as the sense level becomes attuned to this new degree of infusion and becomes able to cope with it: this is like going forward into the room and there meeting the Lord. It is harmless because it is, one could say, occurring in the reverse direction – from spirit to sense. It is only an **overflow** in the psyche from the spirit. It does not therefore have the dynamism of a self-seeking desire, nor does it leave any sadness or depression. There is nothing sinister about it. It merely means that the sensitivity is not yet attuned to the stronger love. If the intimate moment registers as a sexual feeling, it may mean that the Lord is bringing about a healing there.

Let us return to our topic of the journey of prayer:

What is God doing?

The lid is yet again off the subconscious and more **unfinished** business from my past surfaces for me to deal with and to integrate and to be healed of. St John of the Cross speaks of this as a "purification of **memory**" so that I can become better able to be in the **present moment**. This is a preparation for **intimacy** with the Lord, for all intimacy is present-moment-ness.

I see that I am still like a **child,** rating other people with myself as **reference point**. I see people in terms of how they please me or displease me, but not as how they are in themselves. I am still wrapped up in myself. I need to face into relational pain if I am to see others through the eyes of Jesus.

I **pray** at the level of faith; I am called to **live** also at the level of faith. Prayer is like a dance: so also is life. Barry & Connolly write:

> "*As life affects us, God affects us, and as we react to life we react to him.*" [31]

As I say "yes" to life, I say "yes" to God. This is a faith perspective, and we are called to grow in it. The Prayer of Faith enables us to see what faith sees.

Dom John Chapman describes this eloquently:

> We have to learn in practice what we always knew in theory: everything that happens is God's Will. God's Will always intends our good. God's Will is carving us into the likeness of His Son.
>
> Every moment is the message of God's Will; every external event, everything outside us, and *even every*

involuntary thought and feeling within us is God's own touch. We are living in touch with God. Everything we come in contact with, the whole of our daily circumstances, and all our interior responses, whether pleasures or pain, are God's working. We are living in God – in God's action, as a fish in the water. There is no question of trying to *feel* that God is here, or to complain of God being far, once He has taught us that we are bathed in Him, in His action, in His Will. (John Chapman, *Spiritual Letters*. London: Sheed & Ward, 1989. p.143)

> *"No matter how dark the tapestry God weaves for us*
> *there is always a thread of grace."*
> (A Hebrew saying.)

Concluding Prayer

> *Father in heaven,*
> *God of power and Lord of mercy,*
> *from whose fullness we have received,*
> *direct our steps in our everyday efforts.*
> *May the changing moods of the human heart*
> *never blind us to you, source of every good.*
> *Faith gives us the promise of peace*
> *and makes known the demands of love.*
> (31st Sunday in Ordinary Time)

Chapter 8
Growing Further

"My child, if you aspire to serve the Lord,
prepare yourself for an ordeal...
Cling to him and do not leave him...
Whatever happens to you, accept it,
and in the uncertainties of your humble state, be patient,
since gold is tested in the fire, and the chosen in the furnace of humiliation.
Trust him and he will uphold you, follow a straight path and hope in him."
(*Ecclesiasticus* 2:1, 3-6) (NJB)

In the previous chapter, we spoke of a further development in
the Prayer of Faith. It is linked with the wedding intimated by
John the Baptist, the **union** between the baptised Christian and
Christ, the Bridegroom. This wedding would be the flowering of
the **seed** of union that was bestowed in baptism. Jesus now moves
closer to take over more of the life and prayer of the person. In
prayer, there is a greater **shift** to the level of inner experience. A
sense of surrender is given; it feels like floating; it is **interpreted**
by faith to be the felt closeness of Jesus. It is picked up in the
sense of touch, though the **direct** closeness is below the level of
sense. It is **indirect** experience of God. The sense of touch is the
primary sense, and God uses it, at the sense level, to communicate
his closeness at the deeper level. One encounters the **freedom**
of God in this prayer, and learns to adapt to it so as to desire
God rather than God's consolations. One's own freedom, when
ungenerous, can **narrow down** one's openness to God's intimate
communication. And one can, by driving oneself, place oneself
beyond picking up God's closeness. So, there is a call for **balance**
between the drive of desire and what is right for the body.

A new part of the long journey of Prayer of Faith has begun. Essentially it is about **surrender** to the Lord in love. God is

making space for himself in the prayer and the daily life of the person. In prayer, I learn to **receive** and to **let go**. Variation in my experience of prayer, though hard to bear, **trains me** in the art of surrender to how God wants my prayer experience to be. Because we are embodied spirits, God's deep-down loving inflow, when it is stronger than usual, tends to register in the body. I learn that my reaction in my body is not the important thing, and that what really matters is God's hidden love which abides even when not experienced. We learn, when prayer becomes intense, how to let ourselves go into mystery. An **image** in prayer can function as an echo or overflow of what is going on in a hidden way in one's depths, and it reassures us that the Lord is close and all is well. Sexuality may feature in this intimate prayer.

I **pray** at the level of faith. I am called to **live** also at the level of faith. As I say "yes" to life, I say "yes" to God. This is a faith perspective. The Prayer of Faith enables me to see what faith sees, namely, that we are living in God – in God's action, as a fish in water. We are **bathed** in Him, in His action, in His will.

In this chapter now, we explore the further challenge of Prayer of Faith.

Supported in prayer

The experience of prayer tends to settle down at this stage. I grow used to negotiating this gift of God; I learn to allow God to be master of what happens. I come to prayer with less of ego and with more of a desire to be here on God's terms. "I want to please you. It is you I want, or want to want. I dedicate this time to you because you deserve at least this from me." A sense of surrender in prayer grows and grows, even unto a feeling, at times, of strong engagement on the Lord's part. But yet there are times, also, when prayer is like moving across **a desert**, just surviving, and yet **trusting** that the Lord is still with me. Bare as this experience of prayer can feel, I know I am **supported** by it. It helps me to face into what comes up inside me, the **ordeal** that Sirach, the author of Ecclesiasticus, speaks of.

Eyes of faith in daily life

The focus of concern and challenge moves out now **from** the experience of prayer **to** what is happening in the market-place of my daily life. In my experience of prayer, I am still able to find God. I am faithful to it. But I am challenged to find him, also, in my daily life. It means learning to have **eyes of faith** on what happens. Sharing, as I am, in Christ's **prayer,** I am called to live Christ's life **outside** of prayer, also. But this entails an **ordeal.**

Two levels in Christ's experience: the pattern for us

The experience that Christ had on the cross seems to me to be crucial for understanding the way forward. What he went through there was, from a merely natural and superficial view-point, utterly meaningless and quite wrong. But, at another level, he was finding there his Father and the risen life. In his lowest experience, he found the high-point of his life. Where there was nothing for self, there he put pure love. In the mud, he found gold. In the ultimate defeat, he found ultimate victory.

All this is so because there are two levels, the experiential and the spiritual; that of the senses, and that of the spirit. It is also the sacramental principle, as for instance, the bread-and-wine and the presence they carry. This seems to me to run through all our experience in the journey with God and to God. It is central to our quest for union with God in all our activities, for the Creator is hidden and present in all that he sustains in existence. Jesus found his Father, – or, should I say, was found by his Father? – in the apparent defeat of Calvary.[32]

The two levels are evident both in the growth of prayer and the growth in ordinary life outside of prayer, the 'market-place'. We have seen already how the levels feature in the onset and development of prayer of faith – the letting-go at a surface level and the descent into a hidden spiritual level, that of desire and attitude.

While the friendship with Christ in prayer is growing, there is a corresponding growth required in the friendship with him in everyday life. The person I am in my daily life is the person I am in my prayer. The growth of prayer hinges very definitely on the growth in me as a person. Development in the prayer will be the **echo** of the development in being. What matters is the kind of person I become. Am I taking on Christ's values?

Ordeal

In Ecclestiacus, Sirach says,

> "My child, if you aspire to serve the Lord, prepare yourself for
> an ordeal."

The ordeal is in the challenge to let go of my **securities**, and to find enough security in closeness to the Lord. I must let myself be stripped of what I rely on so that the Lord will be my heart's love. Can the Lord be **enough** for me? So Sirach directs me to keep the **focus** of my heart on the Lord:

> "**Cling** to him and do not leave him. ... **Trust** him
> and he will uphold you, follow a straight path and
> **hope** in him."

There will be troubles that will test my worth, but I am not to **dodge** them:

> "Whatever happens to you, **accept** it, and in the
> uncertainties of your humble state, be **patient**,
> since gold is tested in the fire, and the **chosen** in the
> furnace of humiliation."

The Lord has chosen me to be close to him, so I will look on the difficulties I encounter as **gifts** from him. They are intended to shape me into someone pleasing to him and to make me ready to hold more of him.

Desires re-directed

Without **desire** in the following of Christ, no progress is possible; the person must want something, and, if there is to be depth, there must be strong desire. Only strong desire can keep him or her going. I am reminded of the ambitious desire of James and John recounted in Mark 10:35-45: Jesus did not criticise their desire for greatness; he **re-directed** it.

It is in the **difficulties** which are inevitably part of a follower's experience that his or her desires are re-directed by the Lord. It is here, especially, that the **two levels** I spoke of earlier come into play. In the case of the person whose way of life is, so to speak, in the "market-place", the struggle to grow will be experienced mainly **outside** of prayer as in the case of the teacher coping with the classroom scene; the parent adjusting to the changed relationship with her children as they grow up and, apparently, away from her; the business of trying to get on with those one lives with and of becoming someone who excludes none and forgives all; coping with the burden of all the unwanted calls on one's time and energies; coping with the sheer weight of living; with failing memory; with one's increasing sense of one's unimportance; with one's decreasing store of physical and psychic energy; with the tension between action and contemplation; and so on.

I think that what one has in all one's difficulties is an unwelcome experience of **self**. This is really what gets under one's skin. And according as one grows as a person, there is **a losing of control** over one's life and an experience of one's **limits**. The teacher, if he is to become an educator, may have to settle for less external control in the classroom. The parent has to allow an adolescent son or daughter to move into independence. In my community and in my other relationships, I have to give up the desire to change others and the demand that they serve my needs.

This **loss of control**, which is really an experience of self being reduced and of desired success becoming unattainable, can be very **bitter**. It invites one to search for some **meaning** and **help** in the example of **Christ** coping with his experience of failure. One must find something **good** in the bitter experience if one is to keep going and continue to be Christian in one's external behaviour and inward attitude. This is found in the level below the surface.

Unless one looks for what Jesus found on **Calvary** – the Father's will and support – one will not find – or be found by

– the Father and Jesus in one's experience of difficulty. In this experience of failure, what one means by "success" must undergo change: one asks what is real "success"? There is a relentless process here of letting-go that is imposed upon one by very ordinary experience. Somehow, if one is to be more and more deeply found by Christ, one must settle for being dragged into a **share** in his negative experiences; one's secret expectation of "paradise now" must melt away. One is being immersed in reality. Christ cannot take me fully into his union with the Father unless I allow him to take me into his experience of saying "yes" to the realities of human living. Self's desires must be **displaced** progressively if one is to be filled by Christ and be drawn by him into the **current of love** flowing between him and his Father.[33]

Purification

God is revealing himself mysteriously. With so much **hidden light** coming in, there is a great increase in unwelcome self-knowledge. The light reveals so much self-interest, so much mixture of **motivation.** Even in prayer one is seeking self: it can be hard to **want** the times of God's apparent absence. To feel oneself to be a failure in prayer is so humbling, especially if one tends to be very conscientious; one wants so much to be a success in prayer.

This new awareness of **inauthenticity** uncovers layer upon layer of self-interest as though one were an onion or a rag-bag. "Who will deliver me from my ego-self?" "What I thought was virtuous has so much of self-seeking in it." "How petty I can be, and yet I am not able to do better." One sees how one should be but is unable to achieve it. It is as if one is looking out through a glass wall and seeing where one ought to be, but being helpless until the Lord lifts one over. "How quick I am to be jealous! Yet I have so much: I should be grateful." The purification has to be done by the Lord; it is received **passively**; it is his gift. The love received during prayer is enabling the person to bear with the pain of this **unwelcome** experience of self, and to ask the Lord to bring about a change. One knows oneself to be so imperfect, and as in need of a merciful Saviour. One learns to hold these two truths together, namely, that God loves me dearly, and that I am a sinner. It is more a matter of **mixed motivation** and **self-centredness** than of sinful acts. Yet it is very painful, for one is being brought to a heightened awareness of **true** love and authenticity. It is a taste of Peter's experience when he said to Jesus, "Depart from me, for I am a sinful man." I face my basic need for salvation: I see that I cannot save myself. I learn experientially that salvation is a gift, that my holiness is a gift. My image or perception of God shifts from Best Friend to that of the Father of the Prodigal Son. I am loved with an unearned love. I am unworthy.

Going deeper

I **pray** at the level of faith: I am called now to **live**, also, at the level of faith. The Lord is drawing my heart to himself in my prayer so that I will also give him my heart in my daily life.

By **faith**, I am recognising that the **darkness** I experience in prayer is his **presence**. This same faith will help me to recognise that the **dark experiences** I encounter **outside** of prayer also bear his hidden presence.

In my deep prayer of faith, God is drawing near. **Outside** of prayer, his nearness is also at work. This nearness now touches other deep places in me where I discover attachments that are **rivals** to my growing attachment to Jesus. It is as if I go down an **inner lift** to a level deeper in myself than before, and encounter there some **dissonance** in my heart. This inner noise comes into my awareness when something happens that threatens my **security** or my sense of **self-worth**. I am upset, say, at feeling ignored or marginalised; at feeling not accepted; at being misunderstood; at finding someone else honoured; at not being the focus of attention; at a taste of failure in my work; at not being consulted; and so on. I come away from such an event eating my heart out; it has touched me to the quick. So I am angry and I can't shake off my upset. It is as if some **goblins** have appeared from my past, issues that I did not face up to, then, and integrate, and that now raise my anxiety and my fear. They **capture** my attention and threaten to **distract** me from the assurance that I am already receiving from the Lord in **prayer**. What draws my attention so compellingly are those feelings from my past that I have **not yet** come to terms with, such as, fear of **loss** and fear of **insecurity**. If I could say "yes" to what I am afraid of, "yes" to my experience of loss, my fear would diminish, and even vanish.

However, when I choose to draw back from the upset to open myself in **prayer**, I find again the peace of the Lord's acceptance of me, and his tender love, assuring me – if **I will hear it** – that all is well. Can I learn from this? Can I let what has happened **coexist** with the Lord's assurance? Can I bear with **some** pain and turn towards the Lord? He is already giving me tastes of his approval, and is inviting me to **trust**.

I am reminded of what Elkanah said to his wife, **Hannah**, who as yet had no child by him and was enormously upset at this. Elkanah loved his wife, Hannah, and he gave her special signs of his love. On their annual visits to Shiloh to worship there, Elkanah would say to her, *"Hannah, why are you weeping? ... Don't I mean more to you than ten sons?"* (I Sam 1:8) Later, she would give birth to the great prophet, Samuel.

In the deeper places in my heart, now exposed, where my attachment to Jesus is growing, I am being asked to let go of my attachment to **what is not God**. I am being asked, *"Don't I mean more to you than what is upsetting you?"* Can I let go of my attachment to feeling secure through lesser things, and find my security, as Jesus did, in my relationship with him and the Father, for I am a daughter or son of God?

God wants me to let go of anxieties and fear of loss, so as to give me more of himself in closeness, and also to be my security, and, indeed, to be what fills my deepest need. He wants to **fill my heart** and to displace my **rival** attachments. For this, he works to heal me, to free me, and to make space in me for his deeper, loving presence.

A **salient characteristic** of this experience of the Dark Night is that one doesn't fully understand what is going on. This is because God is drawing the person deeper to places where he/she hasn't been before; hence there is the impression that one has lost one's bearings. The forward place is one where old securities are being taken away and God is drawing us into a deeper **trust** that all is well. My trust in God is drawing me forward into relying on **who God is** and away from relying on who I see I am. My self-image as someone good and holy and spiritually successful is being taken from me, so that I can rely on a perception of who God is as always loving and trustworthy. So, **in prayer**, my faith is deepened; it is becoming naked, pure, without props, for it is becoming able to do without perceptible echoes, as it were. There is more surrender to **God's control** of my praying.

Outside of prayer, in my daily living, I am also surrendering to **God's control**. I am better able to go with the flow and to adapt to other people. I am brought into reliance on God's mercy. I see my ultimate salvation as unearned gift, not a reward; for salvation is God's achievement in me, not my own. God is more and more accepted as MYSTERY, to be **trusted** completely. On his Cross, Jesus said, "Father, **into your hands** I commit my spirit." My life, too, is in God's hands; **I trust**. Life's ups and downs conspire, in God's providence, to lead me away from identifying myself with my possessions and with people's approval of me, so that my treasure will lie in **who I am** in my core – God's beloved child – and valuing his approval as enough.

Going deeper still: down the lift
The Dark Night has already brought me into places where my motivations are questioned. "Why am I doing what I am doing, either during prayer or in my everyday life? How much is my ego being served?" My heart or core self is complex, and consequently much of what goes on there is hidden from me, until the Lord exposes my inner self by coming close to me in the Prayer of Faith.

But now I am drawn deeper still into a more trying confrontation with my real self in the Lord's gentle, loving presence. It is the Lord's love I meet here, so I keep in mind that I can come to no harm, unless I choose to run away. This is a safe place, if I keep my heart fixed towards the Lord, as Sirach directs me.

In this deeper place in me, **goblins** appear from my earlier experiences of coping with life. They are painful. Fears, insecurities and anxieties come into play, and, being painful, they capture my attention and threaten to **distract** me from trust that the Lord loves me even here. The pain is acute. But there is also an **Enemy** at work seeking to keep me on the **surface** level of myself. We must now consider this.

Chapter 9

Two-Value Systems

"Do not store up for yourselves treasures on earth,
where moth and rust destroy,
and where thieves break in and steal.
But store up for yourselves treasures in heaven,
where moth and rust do not destroy,
and where thieves do not break in and steal.
For where your treasure is, there your heart will be also."
(Matt. 6:19-21) (NIV)

In the previous chapter, we began our consideration of going deeper. I pray at the level of faith: I am called now to **live**, also, at the level of faith. The Lord is drawing my **heart** to himself, not only in my prayer, but also in my daily life. This will entail an ordeal. We saw the **two levels** in Christ's experience as the pattern for our own way forward. He found union with his Father even in the apparent defeat of Calvary. I will find union with Christ even in my own experiences of difficulty, of loss, and of limitation. I will experience threats to my **security** and sense of **self-worth** inviting me to go deeper and find my treasure in God. I will face my fears and my attachments under the guidance of Jesus my Teacher. I will let Jesus re-direct my heart. Here, now, I will look at my life against the background of the meditation of St Ignatius in the *Spiritual Exercises* called **The Two Standards.**

Warfare

Anyone who takes the journey of faith seriously will encounter both an **attraction** to seeking God and God's will, and also the **opposition** of an Enemy that pulls against this attraction. Our life of faith and our pursuit of God's will are going to lead us into a **conflict** with a power of evil. There is **ordeal** here. The Christian journey is **warfare** in the human heart, just as it was for Jesus. Temptation is the lot of his followers, too. There is a constant battle going on between good and evil in our heart and in the world. So, I need to **know** Christ's way and also the Enemy's way. Both Christ and the Enemy of Human Nature – as St Ignatius calls him – are playing on the **desires** of my human heart so as to influence my **choices**.

The **basic temptation** of the Enemy is to keep people on the **surface** of themselves. The Enemy **tempts** in order to trap.

The **basic invitation** of Jesus is to call people to **depth** in themselves. Jesus **invites** in order to make free.

Desire

I am eager for what is good; I will not be tempted by obvious evil or what looks evil. But temptation is subtle. The desires of the human heart can lead me astray. What is **truly** good? The Enemy uses the ordinary, **legitimate** path of human development to keep me living on the surface of myself. The Enemy's tactic is deceptive and clever. He uses what is good, but good only up to a point, as we shall see, to **deflect** my heart from Jesus and his way. This is where I need to hear the teaching of Jesus on the **true** path of human development, the path he himself lived and taught.

The Ordinary Path of Human Development: Two Models

Model (I)
The search for our identity and self-worth

Where do I live?

For much of our life, as we are growing up, we tend to live on the **surface** of ourselves. It is part of the normal path of development. We are looking for a sense of **identity**: "Who am I? Wherein lies my worth?"

(i) In **childhood**, we tend to search for our self-worth in what is **possessed**.

> This is a pre-adolescent stage. For instance, every child has toys, or talents, or says, "My Dad has an important job", or "I am the best at sums," or "I am a better dancer." As a child, I tend to identify with what I have: be it possessions outside myself, or personal talents within myself. My focus here is on **things**, and having them affords me **security** and a sense of **self-worth**. It may be an infant stage, but we don't outgrow it easily. We live in a consumerist society. As adults, we still tend to value ourselves in terms of our possessions: my big house, my university degree, my achievements, and my position of power. They give me a sense of **importance** and **security**. It amounts to telling myself, "I am what I possess." So, "This is mine" becomes "This is me." But the **truth** is that I am **more** than my possessions.

(ii) In the **second** stage, we search for our self-worth in **the approval of others**.

> This is an **adolescent** stage. In this stage, approval from others becomes very important for my self-worth. There is something **good** in this. I need **enough** approval to learn who I am and to accept myself. Experience of disapproval or non-acceptance from my peers can be very painful. We know this from our own adolescent experience. In my adulthood, I don't easily outgrow this stage. The **esteem** of others can still matter **too much** to me. I begin telling myself, "I am what people think of me"; "I am my reputation". I do indeed need

enough approval of others for my normal healthy development, but people's opinion of me is always incomplete; it is never the full picture. So I need not be controlled by what people think of me. For the **truth** is that I am **more** than my reputation.

(iii) In the **third** stage, we search for our self-worth in **self-sufficiency or power or control.**

This is an **adult** stage. In this stage, one becomes able to manage one's life; to earn one's living; to find a role in life, say, marry and have children. There is something **good** in all of that. However, I can **over-identify** with this self-sufficiency, this power. I begin to want to have control in more and more of my life, even in my relationships. As we know, control does not work well in relationships; it can spoil them. "I am powerful" becomes "I make my own rules." As the song has it, "I did it my way." "I am somebody" may become "I don't need anybody." I lose my sense of **proportion** in relation to others and to God. I become the **centre** of my own world. I am trying to take **total control** of my own existence. I have lost sight of my **creaturehood.** This is PRIDE. It is not the **truth** about me.

Legitimate Values

I want to make an important point about all this.

The values involved in my normal human development are **legitimate:** possessions and approval and power are **good in themselves.** I need **some** possessions, especially interior, personal ones, like my abilities. I need **enough** approval in order to learn who I am and to accept myself as of value. I need **enough** control of my life for taking responsibility. However, Ignatius sees this as the place where the Enemy can trap us. In other words, the Enemy uses these legitimate values to trap me. Where is the TRAP?

The Trap

Possessions, prestige and power are good in themselves, as I have said, but the TRAP lies, not in themselves, but in **how I relate to them**. Possessions are good, prestige is good, power is good, but how I relate to them is where I can go wrong. That is where the trap lies. My desire for them can lead me astray. If I **set my heart** on them, I go astray. Ignatius uses the word **"covet"**, which means "strong desire". Let us look at this.

(i) If I **over-identify** with **possessions**, I become **controlled** by what I have.

> I develop a great fear of loss. I become superficial. So the trap for me is that I **stay on the surface of myself**. This is what the Enemy wants. To live as if I am my possessions is an **untruth**. It diminishes who I am. I am MORE than my possessions. Over-reliance on possessions can **distract** me from what is really important and from the truth about myself. My real worth is not in what I own but in **who I am** in God's eyes, **God's beloved**.

(ii) If I **over-identify** with my **reputation**, I become **unfree** to be myself.

> I become **controlled** by what people say and think about me. I become overly concerned with my image, and again I **stay on the surface of myself**. It becomes hard for me to be who I truly am, as I am always trying to conform to what people say about me to win their approval. To base my life on my reputation lacks **truth**. I am MORE than my reputation. Whose approval is really worth having? It is **God's approval** of me that really matters. God loves me for who I am, not for my achievements.

(iii) **Big desire** for possessions and for status leads to **big desire** for power and control.

Ignatius sees a certain progression in these desires. How does this work? If I have many possessions, I will **expect** to be thought highly of. People will envy me and admire me because I have so much. I am a success. From this I will develop an **exaggerated** sense of my own importance. I become competitive. I will feel powerful. I will want more power. I will experience my power as power **over** others rather than power **for** others. I won't take any orders from anybody. I am the boss. I will make my own rules. **I am the centre of my own world.** But I have lost my sense of proportion in relation to people and to God. I have lost sight of my creaturehood. This is PRIDE, and it results in other evils.

Legitimate

The values here are legitimate. It is the normal way we develop, but the Enemy of our Human Nature turns this way into something bad for us by making us get **stuck** at being too eager for **possessions**, too dependent on **approval**, and too **controlling** in my life. These things keep us on the **surface** of ourselves. We keep looking for our self-worth outside ourselves.

Those legitimate values make **obvious sense**. They do bring me on a path of development, but only up to a point. The TRAP lies in **how I am relating to them**. I can desire them too much. When I **over-identify** with them, I become unfree; I enter untruth; and my **full development** as a human person is held back.

My possessions I regard as my **riches**. They afford me a certain sense of **security**.

But these riches bring me, also, a measure of acceptance and approval from others. Because of them I feel respected and valued, and so they bring me **honour**.

So I come to live habitually as one who is saying to myself, "I am the one who has these **riches**; they are **me**. And I am my

reputation; what people think of me is who I **am**."

However, such a mindset keeps me on the **surface** level of myself. My sense of satisfaction and my concerns in life are on this level. But it is shallow and is not the **truth** about me, for I am **more** than any riches I have, and I am **more** than my reputation.

Going deeper: Who am I?

At my core, at the level where God loves me into existence, out of infinite love for me, I am God's beloved child. So, if I am to grow to deeper levels of myself, I must **descend** towards that core level where I am **loved for myself**, and value myself for that, and there find my **truth**.

In order to **descend** below the surface level of my social existence, I would need to **question** what I am **identifying** myself with: I must draw away from those riches and from the honour they bring. This would entail great interior pain. If, on the other hand, I were to stay attached to my riches and the honour that they bring, I would stay on the surface and live a **superficial** life; I wouldn't let the faith level develop in me. However, because I have already been brought into Prayer of Faith, I am already experiencing unease about my picture of myself.

Faith and relationship with Jesus invite me to go below the superficial style of life. Closeness to Jesus always means going deeper, down to the level of **my heart** and what my heart really wants. The person whose prayer is a Prayer of Faith is already well on the way, but will inevitably face **ordeal** here. This ordeal, however, carries **gift**.

Model (2)
The pursuit of happiness

Everybody is seeking happiness. In our quest for happiness, we have **three basic needs**:

    (1) **Security**,

    (2) **Esteem**,

(3) Control/Power.

They are **instinctual** drives in us. These needs must be met **sufficiently** in childhood and adolescence. They are our natural programme for happiness.

If any one of these three needs was **not adequately** met in childhood, we will have a strong drive in adolescence and into adulthood for either security or esteem or control. We will be **compensating** for the earlier lack. There will be some **disproportion** in our need. So, we may find in ourselves a stronger need for either security or esteem or control. This may help us to identify how the Enemy seeks to trap us. The gap, and the compensation for it, will be a cause of pain for us: it will be a place of strong attachment in us to possessions or approval or control. It will be the place of **particular pain** during the Night of Spirit.

The Ordeal and the Gift:

For example: A person tells her story:

> Since this contemplative prayer developed in me, I have become more and more sensitive to what is happening inside me. I feel the Lord's closeness. I know his love and approval. But I have also become more sensitive to how I am experiencing people. I am highly aware of acceptance and non-acceptance, and I put out a great effort to win favour. This has become a great pain and concern for me now. With someone's help, I learned to see that there was something disproportionate in my reaction to what, in actual fact, were small events.
>
> In my early years, my Dad was unpredictable and moody, and I learnt to be on my guard and to behave in such a way that I would draw his approval and favour. My Mum was also coping with how Dad was. So, between them both I had little enough sense of acceptance and security. I was always on the alert.
>
> This is what is going on for me now. I am in a

position of some responsibility. I am good at what I do. But I am plagued by concern that I will be disapproved of. It is an acute pain. I think I am suffering now what I did not face up to then.

However, by contrast, every time I pray, I find the Lord's approval and security. It is gradually lessening my fear of people's disapproval: I am becoming able to live with my fear and to risk disfavour. But the pain is still acute.

Take another example:

Patrick's issue is around control and surrender, or idealism and love.

Patrick has grown up as an idealistic young man, eager for the best, generous, very committed to his faith, and active in the Church. He admires priesthood for its self-sacrifice and for the good that a priest can do for people. Discernment during a retreat turned his heart towards desiring marriage instead, which he has explored, but priesthood still has an attraction that he can't shake off. He has met a woman with whom he feels very much at home, as with no one else. The love is mutual. They share commitment to the faith. There is so much communion between them. But he finds it hard to **trust** his heart as against his head.

Something happened to him when he was two or three years old, which has left a mark. His mother was ill at home, and he was crying out vociferously for her attention. Dad got angry with him and silenced him. Dad should have taken him up in his arms and comforted him and validated in this way his son's natural desire. But what Dad did had the effect of **squashing** his passion. He began to **distrust** his natural feelings. He became a person who turned his energy towards ideal behaviour, seeking the best. In the process, he was listening to the authority **outside** of him. He was not able to hear the authority of his **experience**.

Even when his heart was so strongly satisfied by the love between him and this lovely woman, this **inner** authority of his heart wasn't able to oust the **outer** authority of his idealism. He was in **acute pain**. The issue was not one of goodness but of taking the **risk** that following his heart was the thing to do, and letting go of that other ideal. Friends urged him forward.

He did choose to follow his heart and married, but he has not yet shaken off the idealism that he spent years serving. The deep wound of boyhood is gradually being healed, for he does meet God's love in contemplative prayer, confirming how right it was to be led by his heart and take the risk.

A **third** example may be read in *A Sunlit Absence* by Martin Laird, in chapter seven entitled, "Sharp Trials in the Intellect". The issue for "Brian" was that he had no sense that his father esteemed him for who he was. In order to receive his father's approval, Brian created a mask. But **who** Brian was went completely unnoticed by his father. This erupted with acute and deep pain.[34]

The True Path of Human Development: according to Jesus

Satan, the Enemy of Human Nature, as St Ignatius calls him, uses the legitimate values of the ordinary path of human development, just described, to hold me at the **surface** level of myself and get **stuck** there. He lures me into this TRAP by getting me to set my heart on possessions, prestige and power. He promises me security, esteem and self-sufficiency there.

Jesus, on the contrary, offers me a GIFT. He invites me to **let go** of what I am clinging to for my security and prestige and sense of control, and offers me a **share** in what he has — a different kind of security, a deeper approval, and a growing awareness of who I am as a child of God. He offers me closeness to himself and closeness to the Father.

Change and Loss

Satan promises me security, prestige and power. So, I give my energies to **holding on** to what I have. But then I encounter **change** and **loss**. This is inevitable. I discover, however, that there is nothing in Satan's programme that equips me for dealing creatively with this. I may try to **numb** myself to the pain; or I try to **distract** myself by being busy. And so, I do whatever I can **not to listen** to what my pain is calling me to. I do this because I have already been living habitually on the **surface** of myself. I discover I lack resources for what is happening to me. I have no spiritual vision for handling change and loss creatively. I fail to find the **gift** in this crisis.

But the **way of Jesus** encourages me not to be afraid of trouble in my life, but, instead, to **engage** with it and to discover that this is one of those places in my life where he is, in fact, **waiting** for me. This is already evident in my experience of the Night. We call this the **Paschal Mystery**. He was finding union with his Father in his experience of passion and death, and was moving **forward** into the new life of resurrection. We, too, find union with Jesus in our own experiences of the **Cross**, and we move **forward** into a further share of that new life. We meet him, and he meets us. This is the mysterious presence that faith enables us to perceive.

The Experience of Change

Nothing in our life stays unchanged, for this is human life. We encounter change and loss and other unwelcome experiences. When we are young, life looks like a succession of new experiences, and we are eager for them. But as we grow older, life is more like a succession of endings, for nothing lasts, and we become more conscious of change and of loss. We don't have to be old to have experiences of disappointment; disillusionment; diminishment; unrequited love; dreams not realised; hopes dashed; experience of being let-down or even betrayed; honeymoons that don't last; and failure of various kinds. Difficult change is the common experience. It feels like we are dying a bit each day, or indeed, dying all the time.

Change brings us pain, so we **resist** it. Yet change, with its losses and endings, is unavoidable. Some people get stuck in resistance to change. Others learn to negotiate it well and to go with the flow; they learn from Jesus, and, if they allow the pain to bring them to a deeper level of themselves, they discover a gift there. This is what Jesus has in store for them. When they **let go** of what they had been clinging to, they find a gift. To change is to leave something behind and to cross over to the **other side**. As André Gide wrote, "One does not discover new lands without consenting to **lose sight** of the shore." The teaching and the lived example of Jesus give us the courage to believe that there is something worthwhile on the other shore. Jesus has led the way in showing us how to negotiate change.

The Gift

The greatest gift that Jesus wants to give to us is **union with his Father**, closeness to his Father. This is what he values most **in himself** – that he is the Son, the Beloved. *"You are my Son whom I love; in you I delight."* (Luke 3:23) (REB) *"The one who sent me is with me; he has not left me alone, for I always do what pleases him."* (John 8:29) (NIV) This union of love between Father and Son is the **golden thread** that gave **value** to his passion and death and enabled him to transform an experience that was, from a merely natural and superficial viewpoint, utterly meaningless and quite wrong. Where there was nothing for self, there he put pure love – love for his Father. In the seeming disaster, he was finding his Father.

In the ultimate defeat, he found ultimate victory.

He has come among us to **share** this with us. He wants to transform our experiences. The union with himself and the Father that began for us in baptism Jesus wants to bring **forward** during our experiences in the Night of Spirit. He wants us to know he is inside our experiences; he wants to be **found** there by us. The Night is about finding the **golden thread of love** for Jesus and the Father down at the level that only faith sees.

"Teacher, where are you staying?"

Let us look for a moment at the experience of Jesus when he begins to be sought after. This happened when he returned to the Jordan after his long sojourn in the wilderness. He was radiant after spending forty days absorbing his Father's word of love – "You are my Son whom I love; in you I delight" – and resisting the Enemy's attempts to deflect him from his Father's will. John the Baptist recognised Jesus when he saw him coming **towards** him and began to witness to him from his own experience of Jesus at the baptism. John's followers were listening to this and their spiritual desire was fired up.

> "*I saw the Spirit come down on him like a dove from heaven and rest on him.*
>
> *I have seen and I testify that he is the* **Chosen One of God**."
>
> (John 1:32, 34) (NJB)

Among the disciples of the Baptist who heard this were Andrew and John. The next day, they were standing near John when he saw Jesus again, this time **passing by**, and he directed their attention to Jesus, saying, "*Look, the Lamb of God!*" The two began to walk after Jesus. When Jesus turned round and saw them following, he asked, "*What do you want?*" They gave an answer which, on the face of it, was indirect and evasive: "*Teacher, where do you live?*"

But this reply turns out to be a **great answer**, for it expresses the essence of the Christian spiritual quest, namely, **"Where am I to find Jesus?"** Am I to go somewhere to find him? Or is he actually very close to hand? Is it a place? Or is it about something inside me? Is it a way of relating? Is he present even in my daily life waiting for me to notice him? If so, where in my own life is he present? How am I to meet him?

Jesus replied by inviting them: *"Come, and see."* They spent the rest of that day with him. What they saw and experienced drew them to spend even the rest of their lives with him. They grew in relationship with him and became like him. This is what Jesus wants for us too, namely, to come to him and be with him and to learn from him. Finding Jesus is about relationship with him. What will the Twelve learn from Jesus over the course of their training? What will we learn?

Learning from Jesus

Possessions

The Twelve apostles, listening to Jesus and observing him, will learn that there is a **gift** in sitting lightly to possessions: *"Blessed are the poor in spirit"*. He is teaching them, and his large audience on the mountain, that they are fortunate, for they will descend to their heart and have space there for deep relationship with God. They will have a taste for divine things. He says: *"theirs is the kingdom of heaven."* Instead of material possessions by which to measure their worth and be secure, they will have a share in Jesus' relationship with his Father: the Father will be **king of their heart**, now and hereafter. This is genuine riches. I am invited in here, too.

> A year ago, I had a breakdown in health. I was diagnosed with breast cancer. At first, I was shocked at the news, and disappointed, and then I was angry. It felt like a big loss then even though it turned out that the treatment did work. My prayer became distracted and I was preoccupied with the change until I got the idea that I should accept it. I began to say 'yes' to what had happened for me. I even began to want the way things were for me, and then prayer

settled back into a being-with. I had the impression it was deeper. The Lord was closer. Prayer flowed. I valued this.

Approval, Prestige

They will learn from him how to evaluate approval and prestige. They see him come under criticism and opposition and plotting from the religious authorities. They will hear him recognising a **blessing** here. For he says, *"Woe to you when all men speak well of you, for that is how their fathers treated the false prophets."* (*Luke* 6:26) (NIV) Praise is deceptive: but the opposite of praise – disapproval – gives you an appetite for God's approval. *"How can you believe if you accept praise from one another, yet make no effort to obtain the praise that comes from God?"* (*John* 5:44) (NIV) Jesus tasted dishonour in plenty from people, but he was highly aware of meeting his Father's approval whenever he would open himself in prayer. This closeness to his Father he valued most: *"The one who sent me is with me; he has not left me alone, for I always do what pleases him."* (*John* 8:29) (NIV) We, too, experience God's approval when we experience an open flow of relationship in prayer. We meet Jesus there too.

I had the experience of feeling put down by someone I respected. It was really a small thing, but I felt rubbished by the way this person treated me. I held my pain; I did not hit back. Later, in my prayer, I had the impression that I should say 'yes' in my heart to this hurt. When I did, I was surprised by the consoling feeling I was given. It seemed like joy. I knew that Jesus loved me. This was enough.

Power, Control

Andrew and his brother James, and the other Ten, too, will learn from him to surrender their competitive spirit, to let go of their great desire for positions of **prestige** and **power**. Instead, he will re-direct their great desire away from dominance and into a desire to serve and to be least of all. They will be graced with humility.

"Whoever wants to become great among you must be your servant, and whoever wants to be first must be slave of all. For even the Son of Man did not come to be served, but to serve, and to give his life as a ransom for many." (*Mark* 10:43-45) (NIV)

I was on a committee charged with planning a big meeting of our members. I felt the chairperson was dominant and even defensive. Many times I came up with good ideas that were supported by several of the others, but this man used his dominant manner to make little of them. I felt disempowered. I was angry. But when I brought it to prayer, which now is a prayer of faith in which I have learned to let the Lord be in control, I saw that I could say 'yes' to this disempowerment happening outside of prayer. This brought me peace and I stayed open to the work of the committee. There was something good for me in it all. There was less of ego in me. I felt a freedom. Prayer was quieter. The Lord felt close.

Re-educates my Desire

Observing Jesus and listening to him **re-educates** my own heart, too, to focus on what is truly worthwhile. Instead of letting Satan set my heart on riches, Jesus invites me to **desire poverty** and there find a different security in the riches of closeness to him. Instead of desiring honour/prestige, I am invited to **desire dishonour**, those experiences that deflate my ego, such as, experiences of being passed-over; marginalised; rejected; experiences of opposition; of lack of appreciation; and I am invited, in the dishonour, to taste **his approval** of me. And then, instead of experiencing pride and displacing God from my heart, I will be able to let God be the centre of my heart's desire. I will surrender to him and I will know how important I am to God. I will find myself **graced with humility**. I will be grounded in the truth of who I am, how important I am to God. (Humility means know-ing my place.)

Jesus' values, of poverty and dishonour leading to humility, **don't** make sense at first sight. I need grace to understand them **as** values, and to trust that they lead to **inner freedom** and to **spiritual life**. So, as I grow closer to Jesus in my desire for him, I become **willing to accept:**

- ❦ **Some insecurity**, for I seek my security in the relationship with God;
- ❦ **Some disapproval**, for I value God's approval most of all;
- ❦ **Some lack of control**, for I want to be surren-dered to God's control of me.

Prayer

> God our Father,
> may we love you in all things
> and above all things,
> and reach the joy you have prepared for us
> beyond all our imagining.
> (Old Missal, 20th Sunday)

Chapter 10
The Cross

"Jesus did not come to explain suffering, nor to take it away;
he came to fill it with his presence."
(Paul Claudel)

In the last chapter, I looked at my journey of human development and considered where I could be trapped on the **surface** of myself in some area. I saw in the teaching of Jesus concerning the true path of human development how I am called to grow **deeper** and at what cost. But alongside the cost, there is the **gift** of a growing union with Jesus. Desire for the values of Jesus opens me to the **treasure** of being close to him. Here now I explore his teaching about **sacrificial love**, his habitual attitude of saying "yes" to the Cross in his own daily life and finding union with his Father there. It is his teaching about the **Paschal Mystery**.

Going Deeper:
Meeting Jesus in Experience of the Cross

The Way of Jesus for our true human development involves a letting-go on our part at the surface level of us in order to grow at a deeper level of us. This letting-go opens us and frees us for going deep. This deeper level is **relationship with God**. The question is: **Where** is relationship with God to be found?

Andrew and his unnamed companion asked Jesus a similar question when they said to him, *"Teacher, where do you live?"* Where does Jesus live? What is his home place? Jesus lives in the **union** with his Father. This is his home. He abides there. He is at home there, no matter what may be happening for him, even in his awful experience of his Passion.

Come and See

When Jesus invited them with the words, *"Come and see"*, he was inviting them into **relationship** with him. They would be changed by being with him. They would see in him that his **home place** was his union with his Father: *"The one who sent me is with me; he has not left me alone, for I always do what pleases him."* (John 8:29) (NIV) They were to discover that their own **home place** would be **union with Jesus**: *"Make your home in me as I make mine in you."* (John 15:4) (JB) Union with Jesus would bring them into Jesus' home place, union with the **Father**. They will learn from him that he is **waiting** for them particularly in their experiences of the Cross. The **Cross** is those experiences in life that involve a dying on one's part, a losing, a letting-go; and Jesus teaches them, and us too, that he is present here. Not only is he present, but, in fact, we **meet** him here. We experience a consoling presence. This teaching is called the **Paschal Mystery.**

When Jesus first predicted his passion, death and resurrection to the apostles, they were stunned. Peter took him aside and began to rebuke him. *"Never, Lord!"* he said. *"This shall never happen to you."* Jesus turned and said to Peter, *"Get behind me, Satan! You are a stumbling block to me; you do not have in mind the things of God, but the things of men."* (Matt 16:21-23) (NIV)

Peter's reaction was our own natural refusal to believe there could be anything good about suffering and death. That suffering and death could be of God and could lead to new life was an utter surprise to the apostles. Why should their hero encounter failure and injustice and death? Is he not close to God? Death would surely be the end and not be of God. How could God be in this?

This was the **hardest** teaching for them to accept from Jesus, and the hardest for us, too. Say I experience a breakdown in health; or I suffer failure in my business; or I am not selected for promotion; or am made redundant in my job. How could any of this be of God and bring me to new life? But Jesus **insisted** that this was the forward-moving path for **all** who desire to follow him: "*If anyone wants to be a follower of mine, let him renounce himself and take up his cross every day and follow me.*" (*Luke* 9:23) (NJB)

The Cross for Jesus

Jesus insisted first of all with **himself** that this was the way forward for him: he must face this reality. He feared that the intervention by Peter would deflect him by appealing to his own human fear of what was in store. He could try to escape the suffering by denying the truth of who he was and by compromising with what was not of God. This was one of Satan's temptations in the wilderness revisiting him now, the one to change God's plan. (*Matt* 4:8-10; *Luke* 4:5-8) It was the return of Satan, as promised in Luke 4:13.

Six or eight days later, Jesus takes Peter, John and James with him and goes up onto a mountain to pray. There he opens himself to his Father's delight in him. He lets himself be loved and is taken over so completely by the Spirit of Love that his body is transfigured. There is **no resistance** in him. This absence of resistance is evident also in the attitude of his heart, for he is saying an **unresisting "yes"** to the suffering he knows is before him, his Cross. Here in the peak of consolation he is saying a total "yes" to the reality before him. His "yes" is to the reality of human rejection because the Father wills him to go through this for our sake. We know that this "yes" is the stance of his heart because we are told that during this experience he is conversing with Moses and Elijah about his "departure", his "exodus", which he predicted to the Twelve about eight days previously. He had said, "*The Son of Man must undergo great suffering, and be rejected by the elders, chief priests, and scribes, and be killed, and on the third day be raised.*" (*Luke* 9:22) The Cross is part of the journey opening up before him, and here now in his heart he is saying a full "yes" to it. This "yes" holds him open here on the mountain to his Father's love. This "yes" is so pleasing to the Father that he envelops his Son in consolation; this fullness of love between them is the Spirit of Love. It is striking to note that his "yes" to the Cross brings Jesus to the peak of union with his Father. Surrender to the Cross, surrender to love, "yes" to terrible reality.[35]

It is also worth noting that this "yes" of Jesus to his Passion would have arisen from a **habitual attitude** of sacrificial love already operative in his heart all through his life.

The Cross for us: a habitual attitude of willingness

Jesus knows that this "yes" to the Cross is the life-giving way for us, too. So he insists, *"If anyone wants to be a follower of mine, let him/her renounce himself/herself and take up his/her cross every day and follow me."* (*Luke* 9:23) (NJB)

The Cross is those **ordinary** experiences that irk me or inconvenience me and cut across my self-interest. I am invited to be willing to be discomfited, to bear the pain of personality differences, and to engage with the sheer burden of living. Such experiences occur **every day**. Sometimes, however, the Cross may be a **major** experience, such as a breakdown in my health; or I suffer failure in my business; or my reputation is wrongly injured; or my child develops a serious illness.

Whatever the Cross is for me, be it ordinary or major, it is something in my experience that I am called to face into if I am to find Jesus. This is what he means by *"take up"*: it is already there. This calls for willingness on my part. I am to **want** it, for he is here. Because he is my teacher and my leader, I am willing to **renounce** something in myself, to deny some inclination in me that is self-seeking, and be led by him. He also says *"his or her Cross"*: the Cross in my life is specific to me.

He says *"every day"*, because what is required of me is a **habitual attitude** of willingness. He is leading me into a habitual attitude of **sacrificial love**, the kind of love that a disciple is called to, like Jesus had.

This may sound like unrelieved austerity, but then he says *"and follow me"*. This means that he is **waiting** for me there: this is where he may be found. He is saying that he is in this part of my experience, and that I will be very close to him, and so he is promising me the consolation of his presence, of his support, of the gift of a growing relationship with him. This is far from mere austerity. It is a movement forward into sacrificial love. This consolation may register in me as peace, or as a willingness that surprises me, or an ease in adapting to the inconvenience. But most of all, I **meet** the Risen Lord there.

Meeting Jesus in the Cross

There is a mystery here. This mystery, or secret knowledge, is that Christ is present below the surface. It is the sacramental principle again: the bread-and-wine and the presence they carry. There is the inconvenience or the pain in my surface experience, and, below it, the presence of Christ. As I said earlier in chapter eight, there are two levels, the experiential and the spiritual, that of the senses, and that of the spirit. We speak of "mystery" in the sense that it is a secret that is open only to those who have been initiated. The initiation is by the gift of faith; faith is able to see below the surface event and to accept that Christ is present here giving me more of relationship with him, deepening this relationship.

This teaching is further brought out in two other sayings of Jesus. In John 12:24, he says, *"Unless a grain of wheat falls into the earth and dies, it remains just a single grain; but if it dies, it bears much fruit."* (NRSV) He speaks of two levels. The wheat grain must let its shell crumble in order to release its potential: the outer part dies so that the inner part can grow. Then he goes on to say, as a development of this, *"Whoever serves me must follow me, and where I am, there will my servant be also."* (12:26) If I follow Jesus, I will be close to Jesus. I will find Jesus.

This teaching is brought out in another way in his saying in Luke 9:24: *"For those who want to save their life will lose it, and those who lose their life for my sake will save it."* (NRSV) (This important saying occurs in each gospel, and twice in Matthew, and three times in Luke.) Again, we note that there are **two levels**: diminishment or "losing" at one level, matched by growth or "saving" at another.

The "loss" spoken of is like the **shell** of the wheat grain. It is at my surface level. The "life" there is the kind of life constructed around my superficial desires, which are ego-centred. My **ego-self** wants to have things go my own way without consideration of others; to feel no inconvenience; not to be disturbed in my self-love; to encounter no disapproval; to see my way as always the right way and to insist on it; to be made much of; to be the centre of attention; to put self first; and so on. If I try to "save" this lifestyle by holding on to it, I will discover at death that I have lost everything. Jesus invites me to "lose" or let go of this level of lifestyle **now**, and to hear and make room for my deeper desires. If I don't, my **true self** will be smothered.

I must make room for my **deepest longings**. There is a different kind of lifestyle that fulfils those longings. My true self is ready to suffer inconvenience for the sake of love; to stand up for the truth, even at cost to myself; to hold back from making judgments; to be patient and compassionate; to be sincere in love. My true self longs to love and be loved, to give and receive in a communion of love, and to be known in truth. I must suffer loss at the surface of myself if my **true self** is to survive and flourish and be "saved".

It is worthy of note that Jesus says, *"for my sake"*. Here he is saying that if I enter this process of "dying" and "losing" **willingly**, and **because of him**, I will be in relationship with him there, and find him there, because he, too, is in this process of moving forward. This process is one of those places where Jesus is **waiting** for me. This is a "mystery" that my faith enables me to accept. Jesus is present in what is happening for me if I choose in faith to see what he sees, and engage with it. There is something hidden and something shared.

The Paschal Mystery: Christ's Presence

The way of Jesus is based on the awareness that **below** the surface level there is a level where the **real me** lies. It is the level where I relate with God and God with me. It is the level of my deep desires. It is the level of my heart. It is the level that faith perceives.

In the doctrine of Jesus, there is a **dying** that leads to new growth; there is a **losing** that leads to a **saving**. He speaks of **two levels**: a diminishment at one level, matched by growth at another. This doctrine, which is known as the **Paschal Mystery**, does not make obvious sense: we need grace to understand it. It is called "Paschal" or "Passover" because it refers to his passage through death to resurrection. It is called a "mystery" because "mystery" here means a **secret** that only a disciple knows: the disciple knows it by faith. The secret that the disciple **knows by faith** is what is happening **below** the surface, namely, a movement forward into life, the life of relationship with Jesus, and, at the same time, a meeting with Jesus. There is something **hidden**, and something **shared**. What is hidden is the **growth** in the relationship. What is shared is the **meeting** with Jesus. On the **surface** there is a letting-go, a losing; **below** the surface, and perceived by faith, there is a movement forward in the relationship with the risen Jesus, and, of course, a meeting with Jesus.

No matter what stage one is at in this process, the disciple will **find** Jesus there, because this process of dying/rising, of losing/saving, is his way of growing, and **now** he is doing the growing in me; he is bringing me forward. And so, when I **enter** my own process of dying/rising, of losing/saving, Jesus also **enters** my process and brings me forward. It is **because of him** that I say "yes" to my losses. And it is also **along with him** that I say this "yes". This **mysterious presence** of Jesus in my Crosses is very precious, and it changes the meaning of events that might trouble me otherwise.

The Night of Spirit

When I enter into a **habitual willingness** to engage with the Cross in my life and look for Jesus there, the ordeal of the Night of Spirit settles down. Prayer and life grow to match each other. Surrender to the Lord becomes easier. One writes the Lord a blank cheque. One is more ready to say, "Let it be done to me." One becomes more able to see the truth of the following quotation:

> Christ saw his executioners as agents of his Father's will. We in our turn must learn to see this same will, this same love, in all the circumstances, pleasant or unpleasant, that surround our life.[36]

Prayer

> Lord God of power and might,
> nothing is good which is against your will,
> and all is of value which comes from your hand.
> Place in our hearts a desire to please you
> and fill our minds with insight into love,
> so that every thought may grow in wisdom
> and all our efforts may be filled with your peace.
> (Old Missal, 22nd Sunday)

Chapter 11

Transforming Union

"They (Jesus and the Eleven) went to a place called Gethsemane,
and Jesus said to his disciples, '(You) sit here while I pray.'"
(*Mark* 14:32) (NIV)

In the last chapter, I saw that the **Night of Spirit** brings me face to face with experience of the **Cross** in my daily life. The Cross is those experiences in life that involve a dying on my part, a losing, a letting-go. I discover from the teaching and example of Jesus that the Cross is a place where he is present and **waiting for me**. If I obey his teaching and say "yes" to my Cross by "taking it up", I find it becomes a place of meeting with the Risen Jesus: he is waiting to be invited into my experience by my "yes". There he gives me a deepening share in his risen life. By a habitual attitude of willingness to facing into the Cross, I become more in tune with his own sacrificial love and become like him. It is as if he brings me into himself and loves in me. In this way, I listen to my deepest longings. The **ordeal** of the Night of Spirit settles down. Prayer and life grow to match each other. Surrender to the Lord, though not full, becomes easier, because graced. I try to offer the Lord a **blank cheque**. I **want** to want only what the Lord wants.

Let us look back at the last **three** chapters, taken together. They outline that part of the inner journey, which is called 'The Night of Spirit'. God was going deeper into the person, claiming more of the person's **heart**, and **displacing** the rival attachments and securities. God was working lovingly and gently; yet, some of the pain was acute. It was felt to be an **ordeal**. The person was **letting-go** of possessions that afforded a measure of security, and was **finding** a gift in some experiences of disapproval. She tasted the wisdom of even **desiring** some measure of poverty and of dishonour, as taught by Jesus. She became free of her superficial attachments and began to find a treasure in a growing attachment to Jesus and in having his **approval**. She was coming into more of her own truth as a **child of God**; this is a deep place. Her heart was distended by desire for God.

More and more she was able to say "yes" to her daily experiences of the Cross, for her **focus** was not on the discomfort, but on desiring to meet the mysterious presence of the Risen Lord in that place.

This part of the inner journey goes on for years. Prayer can feel like **survival**, like "hanging in there". One is there in prayer at God's disposal, as much as can be. Full surrender is not given: there is still a sense of **striving**. God seems to be on the outside, and so, one is reaching out, as it were, and drawn out, and yearning. The ordeal of the Night, however, settles down. Prayer and life grow to **match** each other. She tries to offer the Lord a **blank cheque**.

The Transforming Union

In this chapter, now, we explore the **new level of union** with him into which the Lord brings me. It is called **The Transforming Union** by St John of the Cross. St Teresa of Avila calls it "The Spiritual Marriage", and Ruth Burrows names it the "The Third Island".

At some point of God's choosing, and normally after many, many years, a **definite** transition happens: the union goes deeper; the level of **spirit** surfaces into awareness and one senses a **full surrender** happening. The core of the person is taken hold of by the Lord, and the person consents. It is a consent of love that says, "take me". It is as if one is losing something, but one yields. As Ruth Burrows writes, "It is a kind of death that is life, true life."[37] It is a surrender that arises in the core of the person. One cannot **give** the core of oneself: one can only allow it to be **taken hold of**, and it is the Lord who does this. What happens here is beyond my capacity to do: my core has to be taken hold of by Another and to this I give my consent. As Ruth Burrows puts it, "This consent has been given all along the way, an unconditional consent – 'Do with me what you will'." The Lord takes hold, I give my consent: this is the surrender. The **action** belongs to the Lord.

The **prayer** also belongs to the Lord. Prayer, now, arises from the core or spirit of the person, and is experienced as the prayer of Another. Just as the surrender into God is experienced as done in oneself by Another, so also is the prayer experienced as done in oneself by Another, the Risen Jesus. It is sheer gift. It is as if what Jesus said to the Eleven at Gethsemane has come true: "You sit (or stay) here while I pray."

The Transition

The transition into this new place of prayer, where the level of spirit surfaces into consciousness, is experienced variously. A salient feature of each is **recognition**. It is recognition of a **new depth opened**. Here are some descriptions:

One person, who had been living through the experience of bereavement after the death of a very dear friend, said this:

> Prayer continued to be imageless and quiet. It supported me in my loss. A certainty had grown in me that I am deeply loved and, to such an extent, that I was feeling at home in the prayer and had a sense of belonging. Then, one day during prayer, I sensed that my relationship with the Lord had gone deeper. Someone else's words express it for me: 'I felt a **unique intimacy**; I felt touched in my **core**.' I knew that this was different. Now, the Lord's movement in me comes unannounced. I can't turn it on. The touches of his presence seem like a **kiss** in my spirit, so deep are they. There are times now when prayer **finds** me. In prayer I feel **acted** upon. It is dark still, but I find communion there. **Communion** is the best word for me. Prayer seems to continue when I have ended it to do something else.

A woman, already a grandmother, describes a different experience of transition:

> During my retreat, I was at prayer in the chapel before the Blessed Sacrament. I felt an **energy** rising in me. It became very strong. I was overwhelmed by the experience. Something powerful was happening to me. I was being loved intensely by the Lord and taken over. This was new. Prayer was filling me as never before, and I let myself be **taken**. After that, I was conscious of prayer being **done** in me, and I had a great desire for prayer for many days. All I need now for prayer is only to be **idle**, waiting expectantly. The Lord does the praying more obviously than before.

Another person, a priest, describes how this change of depth happened for him:

> It happened during my annual retreat. Looking back, I remember saying a year before to the retreat director, 'I hope I can survive', for that is what prayer of faith felt like after many, many years of it.
>
> And now, this was Day Five of the current retreat. My prayer was habitually imageless, but this afternoon I found myself presented with an **image** of a seashore, where the small waves were washing in as the tide was rising. I was looking at something in the water: was it a piece of wood, I wondered, or was it a very small creature? I became quite involved in what I was watching, wishing for this little creature or thing to make it to land. I became full of compassion for it, as I watched it being nudged forward onto the shore by wave after wave. I wanted very much for it to succeed. And then, it did reach land beyond the final wave.
>
> The image then stopped and I became aware of myself: I felt something was different. I felt prayer

welling up inside me; this was a new kind of prayer. It was a new kind of experience. I could hardly believe it. On the one hand, I was thinking, 'Yes, this is different', and on the other hand, I thought, 'No, it isn't'. I could hardly believe it.

Then, I saw the **meaning** of the image that had unfolded: I was the little creature or thing that had landed on this island after its long journey over the ocean. And I recalled something that I had read a year or more before this: this must be the Third Island, and I have been brought there. I noticed that prayer was happening even when my mind was focused somewhere else: it seemed **independent** of me.

Another person, a Sister, describes what happened in this way: My prayer has been dark and imageless for many years now: it became a simple 'being-with'. It supported me while I was coping with a bout of cancer that I have now mercifully come through, and then it helped me bear with a fracture that happened after a fall soon after that. The 'being-with' in prayer became bare, then, but I still trusted it. I also noticed a change in me to being tolerant of someone and letting her be. Then, one day after Christmas, something new happened in prayer. I had the feeling of finding a treasure, something precious; and during the prayer an image presented itself of a well, and I was looking down into it, and there I saw my own face on the surface of the water. But, while gazing at it, I wasn't thinking about myself. I was just gazing at my face. I felt calm and had a deep peace. This went on for what seemed a long time in the prayer, and was very satisfying. Then, for days afterwards, I felt myself drawn to prayer.

In discussion with my spiritual director afterwards, I understood that, in this metaphor, I was seeing into my own centre, my own depth, where the prayer of Jesus is happening in me now. It was the 'well of life-giving water.'

Another woman experienced this change on Day Six of a directed retreat:

I see what happened for me in a context. I'm a nurse, just retired. In my retreat, I was looking over my professional life with lots of gratitude for how things have turned out for me. I remembered a key time when I put the needs of my patients clearly before my own interests, and how afterwards I realised how much I had grown as a person in doing this. Then, when I retired recently, I was ready to let go of so much of status and security. I am facing an unknown future. In prayer these past days, I sensed that I was being loved by Jesus and receiving strength to face the unknown.

Yesterday, I sensed that Jesus was revealing himself to me, revealing that he is present, but without any image, and that he loves me. I was resting in his presence; it was a growing experience of love. I felt a warmth, and was accepting this, not drawing back.

Today, I was on my own in the chapel and felt a 'unique' experience. Prayer was very quiet at first, but then I felt overwhelmed by love, a received love, an energy. I found myself speaking my love to him and told him that he was the central support in my life. I felt myself opened in a new and deeper way. I am in a deeper place in myself. During the next prayer time, which was after supper, I felt caught up in this love. But then, in the next two times, prayer was very quiet.

The Prayer

In this prayer, God's action is by-passing, not only the level of words and images, but also the intellect. One is confronted by Mystery. It is God-without-image. It is a share in the prayer of Jesus. There is no striving now; the self's intensity is gone, for it is Another's intensity that is felt.

This prayer is experienced, not as coming from outside, but as welling up from within. It is as if God is "waking up in the innermost centre".[38] As André Loaf puts it, prayer is "welling up". People describe their experience of this prayer as "a stirring within".

Jean Pierre de Caussade SJ wrote, "There is a time when the soul lives in God, and a time when God lives in the soul."[39] "The soul lives in God": God is, as it were, on the outside. This fits the experience of the Prayer of Faith. "God lives in the soul": God is, as it were, inside. This fits the new experience of union now given, called Transforming Union. God is inside, and the self in prayer is displaced: God has taken over in the core depth of the person that is termed "spirit"; it is the innermost centre, the level below the spiritual faculties of intellect and will. God has moved in, and a new inner journey has begun. God has taken hold of the person's self in a permanent way. It can be painful to experience such helplessness in prayer and the displacement it entails. Nevertheless, it is consoling to know that the Lord is so close. It is a marriage of wills.

Ligature

Awareness of the level of spirit is **indirect**. God is acting **directly** at the level of one's spirit, but one can be aware of this active presence of God only **indirectly** through the reaction experienced in one's body. In one's body, one feels acted upon, quietened, made still, caught up in adoring focus, filled with love, and even unable to speak a prayer and know its meaning.

This inability is called "**ligature**", from the Latin word for "to bind": the soul is so occupied with God's action being received

that it cannot at the same time be active; it is bound, constrict-
ed. It means simply that one cannot put one's mind to do two
things at once, and if the intellect is occupied with God, it cannot also practice meditation on a subject: the received focus on
God interferes with a focus on meaning. "The experience is like
that of being unable to understand what one person is saying,
because we are intently listening to another; only in this case, that
of prayer, there is the distraction without any consciousness of
what causes the distraction, namely, the engagement with God.
The intellect is tensely engaged in seeing something invisible,
looking at a black night, listening to silence, speaking to someone who is not there – these are symbolic phrases, – and cannot
do its ordinary work."[40]

The experience of "ligature" will have already featured during
Prayer of Faith, but now, during Transforming Union, it is likely
to feature more. For instance, one may find during Mass that
one is drawn mysteriously beyond awareness of meaning at the
Eucharistic Prayer and be unable, except with great effort, to follow the meaning of the words being spoken by the celebrating
priest. One feels one is losing something important. But, in fact,
far from losing, one is being brought beyond the words to the
mystery happening there, the surrender of Jesus to the Father in
adoration and love, and one is being drawn to be there with Jesus.
The sense of great effort to follow the meaning is a **sign** that one
is to let go of the meaning. One must **go with** the loss of focus
on meaning and accept one's participation in mystery. The same
experience of "ligature" can happen, say, when the congregation
are reciting the "Our Father": one feels displaced within and
unable to be with the meaning of the words. But, in fact, one is
more connected with what is being expressed by the others.

The Prayer of Another
Prayer is now experienced as the prayer of Another. It is a wholly
received prayer. **All** the work is done by God. In order to let this
prayer surface into awareness, all that one needs is to slow down

one's body and become idle and let the prayer arise. It is an idleness that is like **anticipating a visitor.** The prayer is like, "See, he comes", and being sure of his coming. The person has become the **space** for Another's praying: it is the prayer between Jesus and the Father. The person is **carrying** prayer.

Prayer is going on all the time in the depths. In the depths, it is like a **pilot light.** This insight comes from what someone shared. He said:

> When the alarm sounded, I found that I wasn't ready to get up. I also noticed that I was in prayer. Now I was realising that my unreadiness for getting up was due to this very quiet prayer. It felt so close to me that I found myself thinking, 'I am the prayer of Jesus.' Then, an **image** presented itself of me holding a liquid-gas lighter, like the ones we have for lighting candles. It was alight. I tried to turn it off, but there seemed to be something wrong with the mechanism, for I could not turn it off. It continued showing a small flame. Then, I saw that this was about the **prayer** in me. It was telling me that it was always on, and that it was the prayer of Jesus inside me. So, it reminded me of the '**pilot light**' or 'glimmer' in a gas-fuelled cooker or heater always on, and turned up into a full flame whenever required for cooking or heating.
>
> At another time, before I got up, I found myself experiencing union, and I was aware of myself again as **being** the prayer of Jesus. Then I saw that I am also called to **be** the **compassion** of Jesus, the love of Jesus, the patience of Jesus, and so on; in other words, that he wants to **express** himself through me. This feels quite daunting. But it does make more sense to me of the union with Jesus as a call to be 'another Christ'.

The person has only to be **idle,** in the sense of **expectantly wait-**

ing, for prayer to assert itself in consciousness. So, trying to **make** prayer can block this full prayer, for the prayer itself is God's action in the person.

Trying to pray is like attempting to take back control, but it won't work. This prayer is wholly a received prayer: the person yields to it, surrenders to it. It takes time for the person to trust that she need not, and indeed must not, try to **make** prayer. It may seem a simple thing just to be idle in an expectant way in order to receive prayer, but negotiating this space feels like one is walking a **tight-rope,** trying to find the balance between being present and not interfering. One is on the two levels of spirit and body, and walking the balance between them is not easy. One learns that this again is not something I do, but something I **receive.**

One person had this insight into how to negotiate the inflow of God's active presence:

> I am probably more self-aware than many people, so I find myself in prayer inclined to **monitor** the experience and find words to **capture** what is happening in me. But I sensed that this was in the way of my engaging fully in the experience of the union being given. I discovered that what helps me now is to regard the experience in prayer as happening to **someone else**. It is like a looking away from the experience. This liberates me from monitoring it or from looking for words to formulate what is happening. Seeing it as someone else's experience takes me out of the way, as it were, and enables me to surrender **blindly** to what God is doing. I can become more or less lost to myself and flexible to God's gift. I am not sure why this works. I think it is that I am enabled to go along with the displacement better, and I have a sense that I am less there and yet more there, at the same time.

Self-transcendence

This prayer involves **self-transcendence**, a yielding to Another: ego-self is being **displaced**. It is Christ's prayer within the person. The person is sharing in Christ's adoration of his Father and in the Father's love for his Son. This interaction is the Holy Spirit, the bond of love between them. There is **no content** to focus on, for God is here as Mystery, but there is attitude, such as adoration, awe, surrender, deep desire, love.

A New Journey

A new journey has now begun, and a further purification, in accordance with God's intention for this person, can come. Much suffering will have preceded this new beginning already, and there may be more to follow; but it will be as part of union with Christ, such as the great darkness of faith experienced by St Thérèse of the Child Jesus, for the sake of the Church, in the final year of her life. St John of the Cross calls this prayer level a "**transforming** union", not a "transformed union", for God's work is not all done yet.

Substantial touch

It is a wholly **receptive** and passive prayer. Prayer can be perceived to be going on while the mind's attention is only partially engaged with something else. The level of spirit is a deep, deep place, and sometimes the person can pick up in bodily awareness a sense of a deep touch, happening at a level of spirit, the impression that something like a ray is reaching into the profound depth that is there. One's spirit is being touched mysteriously and beyond direct perception, but one's body reacts, and it is this reaction that is perceived and interpreted. This is called a "**substantial touch**", meaning a touch at the foundational level below intellect and will. Often the surface of oneself can be drawn inwards, down towards the deep centre, in great absorption and great quiet, and finding a great stillness: it is this quiet that tells one that God is active mysteriously below the great quiet. Sometimes, one can become lost to oneself, and drawn into an un-awareness of self as praying.

The grace of baptism

So, the last level to surface into consciousness is the **first** that was touched by **baptismal grace**, namely, the person's deepest centre. Therefore, this new level is just the **flowering** of the grace of baptism, which implanted the seed of the presence of Father, Son and Holy Spirit in the soul. It surely is God's great desire for us that this foundational grace should take root and grow and flourish into a developed faith. This transforming union is a **new beginning**, the start of a new journey that is endless – even till death – for God is infinitely deep. The One who is transforming those he has touched is himself an abyss of endless depth where the journey of transformation need never cease. This abyss is the loving embrace of Father and Son, who can draw us ever more deeply into their current of love who is their Spirit – on and on and on.

Outside of Prayer

There is likely to be an **authenticity** about this person, a congru-ence or matching between the inner self and the presented image: "what you see is what you get". Ego-self has been very much faced up to. The person's uniqueness emerges, and is trusted by her. A lot of integration has come. The sexual drive, too, is more integrated. Such depth of intimacy with God, who is love, goes hand in hand with a capacity for intimacy with friends.

Outward living is **ordinary**, nothing special: the two levels again, the gold hidden in the ore, as mentioned in Chapter Eight. Daily life continues to be ordinary, unimportant, but what is below the surface is **extraordinary**. Indeed, the same could be said about any **baptised** person who is living a life of faith: on the surface things are ordinary, but, below the surface, the Trinity find their dwelling here. But for the person whose prayer has developed into the transforming union, there is an **awareness** of this presence and action. It is the little people who are gifted with this deep intimacy. Fruitfulness is evident, too: God is working through this person.

The Experience of Prayer

One person, a priest, shared what his experience of prayer in the Transforming Union is like:

> The experience varies a lot. There are times when the sense of engagement that is given seems light, but I always trust that the prayer is going on inside me in a hidden way. Many times I feel myself caught up and filled with some energy or presence: it is hard to describe. The sense of being filled is also like a sense of being **displaced** by a presence, but the presence is more like an absence: I feel displaced, pushed back, emptied, brought to some kind of limit of stretching, and in this state I am speechless; I can't join actively with the others at Mass. I am taken over, but there is no consoling feeling in it. But I know that it tells me that God has deep access into me, and it is this realisation that consoles me: that there is no barrier between us.

Another person, a Sister, expressed the experience this way:

> A memory came back to me of my parents when they were elderly, sitting at either side of the fireplace, saying nothing. I was seated between them, in front of the fire. Though no words were being used, I sensed a **communion** between them. Dad was looking at the newspaper, but I knew that they were present to each other, nevertheless. This is what my prayer experience is like – I am picking up the **silent communion** between the Father and the Risen Lord inside me.
>
> In retreat time, it is a loving being-with. There is

a silent communion, a very deep peace, and a resting peacefully in the Presence. There is never an image. The deep peace in my feelings is the effect of what is happening deep down. Outside of prayer, I can be moved by, say, a text of Scripture, such as, 'My delight is in you.' (*Isaiah* 62), or 'The Lord will do the fighting for you; you need only to be still.' (*Exodus* 14:14) My experience inside prayer is dry but loving.

Another person, who is a widow, shared this:

I was making the *Spiritual Exercises of St Ignatius in Daily Life*. At one stage, I found myself **letting-go** in prayer. I had been reflecting on scripture, and saw there that Jesus, and Mary, his Mother, had **let go** on Calvary. Prayer became very quiet; I felt lost; I was tranquil. I was saying, in my heart, a 'yes for now', not a 'yes for an unseen future'. It was a kind of surrender. I remembered what happened about two years after my husband's death. It was in Lough Derg. I wasn't asking for anything, but suddenly I felt peace and a release. I realised that it wasn't I who surrendered: I had **received** surrender. I didn't do it: it was **done** in me. I saw that Jesus had been present to me at every crisis. He enabled, and will enable, whatever surrender he wants of me. I will be able to accept whatever he allows to happen.

One morning in bed, a few weeks later, just as I was waking up, I found myself realising, '*I am the pearl of great price*'. I **knew** it. It was a wonderful feeling. Jesus has purchased me; he has paid the ransom, because he wanted me so much. So, he is making it easier for me to say, 'Take and receive'. At Holy Communion, **he** says to me, 'Take and receive' Me.

A little while later, I remembered some early experiences. At age 6 or 7, I was at the window and I felt an inner touch. I never told anyone about it. At 14 or 16, I was on a swing and felt something deep inside me. I felt a joy for no reason. Again, I told nobody about this. It comes back to me now when I realise that I am the 'pearl of great price'. I feel a bubbly joy, an excitement.

Prayer is **effortless**. It is like **snorkelling** below the surface – not deep below – and not thinking. Sometimes, it goes deeper. My gift in prayer-time is the **time** itself: letting Him engage my attention. I don't see prayer as my gift to God.

I am still learning to pray, namely, that I am to **let** prayer, not make prayer. Prayer is like basking in sunshine.

Another person, now a grandmother, expressed it this way:

Prayer now is like sitting in his shadow, contented, and having a sense, at the same time, that there is stream running underground. Prayer is so quiet. I know when to make a transition out of this prayer: it is when there is what I would call 'a spent feeling.'

Fr Iain Matthew OCD, writes of what he surmises was the usual experience of St John of the Cross in prayer:

What kind of visitation? John can speak of an encounter with the divine which takes one's breath away. But he relishes more a presence that emerges from within, from behind; as if one entered a dark room, and sat there on one's own... then, after some minutes, yes there is someone there, has always been, a silhouette becoming clear. There, 'in the midst' of obscurity, John speaks of 'a kind of companionship and inner strength which walks with the soul and gives her strength' – a presence that is gentle, imperceptible, 'dark', which evaporates if John tries to describe it but which sustains his life. That is the visitation.[41]

Droopy little bits of green

The person in the state of transforming union is looking **to-wards** God in love and is looking **to** God for the support she needs for doing his will. She is aware of his merciful acceptance of her as she is. But sometimes, she looks back at herself and sees that she is not measuring up to some ideal image of herself. She sees that she is not perfect, and begins to worry that her occasional feelings of annoyance, antipathy, jealousy, reluctance to please, contrariness, are displeasing to God and should be eradicated. But when she is asked in spiritual direction if any of that is obstructing the flow of union between her and God during prayer, she sees that the flow in the experience of union is telling her that all is well and that the other experiences do not matter at all. What Ruth Burrows says here in this regard is very helpful:

> The **roots of sin** are cut, but maybe some **droopy little bits of green** are still there – feelings of jealousy, annoyance, contrariness, but they are absolutely harmless, mere feelings, rather like those that remain when a limb has been amputated. She does not ask them to go, because she knows they do not matter... She does not have to struggle against these feelings; they are there to keep her holding out her hand to Jesus.[42]

Through her endless surrenders leading up to this place, she has become firmly set towards God and God's will, and is now confirmed in that grace. So, Ruth Burrows can say, "The roots of sin are cut". These shortcomings become **gifts** to her, keeping her humble.

Total Surrender

Saying "yes" to the **Cross** in one's life becomes more and more a feature in this level of union. This person of the transforming union has been drawn into a share of the **surrender of Jesus to his Father**. It is a mystery we celebrate at every Mass, and there we receive grace to yield further to the Lord, to the degree that the Lord may want. I would like to quote again the words I quoted in Chapter One about Fr Pedro Arrupe SJ, whose illness drew him into a profound surrender, as described in the words his close assistants drew from him. Arrupe was then General Superior of the Society of Jesus. He had been able to speak in sixteen languages, but now he was in a wheelchair after a stroke and able only to hint, through his native Basque language, at what he wanted to communicate to his fellow-Jesuits.

> More than ever, I now find myself in the hands of God. This is what I have wanted all my life, from my youth. And this is still the one thing I want. But now there is a difference: the initiative is entirely with God. It is indeed a profound spiritual experience to know and feel myself so totally in his hands.[43]

Conclusion

Contemplative prayer is never mastered, for God, who gives prayer, is always greater. In prayer, one dances with the Lord, who leads the dance. The experience of prayer registers in the bodily senses, and so, the experience will vary according as to whether one is tired or alert or anxious or at peace, and so on. It will also vary with what the Lord chooses to give in the moment, such as a surge of love, or a profound silence, or a taste of awe, or a simple presence, and so on.

The important thing is the relationship with God, and this is 24 hours a day. The shape of one's prayer will arise from the shape of the relationship.

Metaphors

The prayer described in this book is best conveyed by metaphors, such as, energy; an ocean; emptiness; oneness; a kiss; a visitation;

following a scent; a fragrance; a wounding; a desert; an embrace; a holding; an embrace from behind; a floating; a searching; an awakening; entering a magnetic field where everything gets righted, like iron filings do.

Prayer has already begun in me

I have said before that the prayer I have been describing in this book is a **flowering** of the grace implanted in us at Baptism. These words by André Louf, O Cist express this powerfully:

That place where God dwells in me is also the place of prayer. Long before I am aware of it or before I take an interest in it, this prayer is going on **ceaselessly** within me. In effect, it is not I who gives myself to prayer, but the **Holy Spirit** who never ceases to pray in me with inarticulate groans, as St Paul says in his Letter to the Romans (cf 8:26).

This prayer is my heart's treasure. It is a hidden treasure which is buried in the deepest part of my being, access to which is presently obstructed by a host of realities which distract me from prayer. These tend to keep me at a superficial level of my being... and cause me to lost contact with the fire smouldering within me.

It is important to insist on this: right from the beginning, prayer has **already begun** before I do anything – it comes before any of my efforts or techniques. From the moment when I received the life of God in **baptism**, prayer has been **poured** into my heart along with the Holy Spirit who was then given to me. (*Rom 5:5*)

Prayer is there; it **abides** there. The Holy Spirit in person intercedes there for me and for all the saints. It is he who celebrates an unceasing liturgy, who makes the voice of Christ my voice, who lifts me up before God...

'To live in a state of grace', means that at a deep level I live in a **state of prayer**.

At the beginning this prayer is entirely unconscious, so all my efforts will consist in **letting** the prayer flow out and spill over into my consciousness. Nothing more than that. From being unconscious, this prayer must become **conscious**. I must **allow** it to take me over from within, so that I can become united with it, and take direction of it, while allowing myself to be borne up by it.[44]

Chapter 12

Becoming the Love of Jesus

"I give you a new commandment,
that you love one another.
Just as I have loved you,
you also should love one another.
By this everyone will know that you are my disciples,
if you have love for one another."
(John 13:34-35) (NRSV)

In the previous chapter, we explored the new level of union with the Lord that is called 'The Transforming Union'. The transition into this union is variously experienced. A salient feature is the **recognition** by the person of a new depth opened. This depth is the level of spirit below the level of intellect and will: it is the core of the person. A full surrender into the union with the Lord is experienced. This union is the Lord's gift to which the person consents. Prayer, now, in the person, belongs to the Lord: all the work is done by God.

This union is a **new** beginning in the relationship with the Lord. The prayer **arises** from within. It is God's **direct** action at the level of spirit, an action which is perceived **indirectly** through the reaction in one's body, such as peace, love, awe, absorption, stillness. It is the prayer of Jesus, the Risen Lord, engaging with his Father. It is a wholly **received** prayer done by God, and all that one needs to do is to slow down one's body and become **idle** in a way that looks forward to his visitation: this is an expectant idleness.

It is a union that is 'transforming'. So, this prayer is **never mastered**, for one encounters the freedom of the Lord whose concern is to draw the person forward in a deepening relationship for the sake of the Church. Consequently, the experience

varies. This union is the **flowering** of what began in baptism. Just as with baptism, outward living may appear **ordinary,** but what is below the surface is **extraordinary:** the indwelling of the Trinity. This must necessarily **overflow** in fruitfulness for the Church in some way: *"This is to my Father's glory, that you bear much fruit, showing yourselves to be my disciples."* (John 15:8) (NIV) Saying "yes" to the **Cross** in one's life becomes more and more a feature in this level of union.

Becoming Christ's Prayer, Becoming Christ's Love

In this chapter, we focus on the desire of Jesus that we be **bearers of his love.**

During the journey of Prayer of Faith, Jesus has been moving in to take over our prayer so as to be the One who **prays** in us. During Prayer of Faith, Jesus has also been at work to **redirect** our heart, so as to be the One who **loves** in us, who forgives, who is patient, who bears the Cross of daily interaction with our neighbour. He takes over our praying, but also our heart, to give us **his own heart.**

In Chapter One, I quoted a saying of Evagrius of Pontus: "If you want to pray, you need God who **gives prayer** to the one who prays." This saying may be extended to include love and forgiveness and service, and all the qualities that mark a disciple of Jesus. "If you want to love, you need Jesus who **gives love** to the one who loves, and so on."

This was the great insight that St Thérèse of the Child Jesus had into Jesus' new commandment in John 13:34-35 and John 15:12. It was during the time of her trial of faith as described in her *Story of a Soul,*[45] in the third part, which was addressed to her Prioress, Mother Marie De Gonzague. She was pondering deeply on the commandment of Jesus that we are to love one another as Jesus has loved us: "A new commandment I give you, that you love one another: that as I have loved you, you also love one another. By this everyone will know that you are my disciples, if you have love for one another." (John 13:34-35)

A New Commandment

Thérèse was recognising that this was a **new** commandment. The **old** commandment was that people love their neighbour as themselves (*Lev* 19:18). She observes:

> When the Lord commanded His people to love their neighbour as themselves, He had not as yet come upon the earth. Knowing the extent to which each one loved himself, He was not able to ask of His creatures a greater love than this for one's neighbour. But when Jesus gave His Apostles a new commandment, HIS OWN COMMANDMENT, as He calls it later on (*John* 15:12), it is no longer a question of loving one's neighbour as oneself but of loving him as *He, Jesus has loved him*, and will love him to the consummation of the ages.

Command and Promise

This is the place where Thérèse is graced with a most helpful insight. She sees that such love, to love as Jesus loves, is beyond her capacity, conscious as she is of her weakness and imperfection. But Jesus has **commanded** this kind of love for one another. So, her insight was that, along with the command, comes the **promise** of the grace for doing this, that is, for loving as Jesus loves. She says, "Ah! Lord, You know very well that never would I be able to love my Sisters as You love them, unless *You, O my Jesus, loved them in me*. It is because you wanted to give me this grace that You made Your *new* commandment." She saw that Jesus' promise is to be **inside** her doing the loving. She exclaims, "Oh! how I love this new commandment since it gives me the assurance that Your will is *to love in me* all those You command me to love!"

Working with the Love

Then, she goes on to say that she **experiences** this love in her:

> Yes, I feel it, when I am charitable, it is Jesus alone

who is acting in me, and the more united I am to Him, the more also do I love my Sisters. When I wish to increase this love in me, and when especially the devil tries to place before the eyes of my soul the faults of such and such a Sister who is less attractive to me, I hasten to search out her virtues, her good intentions; ... I tell myself that even what appears to me as a fault can very easily be an act of virtue because of her intention.

She is well aware of her inclination to focus on the faults of others, and she **leans against this** by hastening to search out the good points in them and to presume good motivation in them.

Thérèse speaks of a Sister in the Community:
who had the faculty of displeasing me in everything, in her ways, her words, her character, everything seems *very disagreeable* to me. And still, she is a holy religious who must be very pleasing to God. Not wanting to give in to the natural antipathy I was experiencing, I told myself that charity must not consist in feelings but in works; then, I set myself to doing for this Sister what I would do for the person I loved most.

So, she set herself to praying for her often. She also did more:
I wasn't content simply with praying very much for this Sister who gave me so many struggles, but I took care to render her all the services possible, and when I was tempted to answer back in a disagreeable manner, I was content with giving her my most friendly **smile**, and also with changing the subject of the conversation. ... Frequently, when I was not at recreation (I mean during work periods) and had occasion to work with this Sister, I used to run away

like a deserter whenever my struggles became too violent. As she was absolutely unaware of my feelings for her, never did she suspect the motives for my conduct and she remained convinced that her character was very pleasing to me. One day at recreation she asked in almost these words: 'Would you tell me, Sister Thérèse of the Child Jesus, what attracts you so much towards me; every time you look at me, I see you **smile**?' Ah! what attracted me was Jesus hidden in the depths of her soul; Jesus who makes sweet what is most bitter.

Note that Thérèse **works** with the **grace of love** given to her: and she works **against** her natural antipathy so as to **release** the gift of love in her.

Working with the gift

We know something, too, of what it is like to **work** with the **grace of prayer** being offered: we work **against** our natural inclination to put self first and to maintain control and to cling to our own will. Similarly, we are invited by the Lord to **work** with the **gift of love** being given to us. When, as disciples of Jesus, we truly love, it is with the love that Jesus is giving us; when we are truly patient, it is with his patience in us; when we take up our Cross each day, it is with his sacrificial love that we can do this. We cannot be like Christ unless we **release** the gift he is giving us of being loving, patient, considerate, affirming, forgiving and so on. We have already become the **prayer** of Jesus: we are invited to become also the **love** of Jesus.

Prayer

Dear Jesus, help me to spread your fragrance everywhere I go.

Flood my soul with your spirit and life.

Penetrate and possess my whole being so utterly

that all my life may be only a radiance of yours.
Shine through me and be so in me
that every soul I come in contact with
may feel your presence in my soul.
Let them look up and see no longer me but only
   you, O Lord.
(Blessed John Henry Newman)

Part 2

FOR SPIRITUAL
DIRECTORS

Chapter 13

Discerning Contemplative Prayer

Discerning whether a person is **entering** contemplative prayer comes down to discerning the **dryness** that is the **transition** into it. For the dryness can be **negative** or **positive**. If *negative* it is not the transition.

A. Positive dryness

Presuppositions

For dryness in prayer to be **positive**, a certain growth in prayer and in our lived relationship is **presupposed**.

Say the person has moved through the **stages** of meditative prayer and then imaginative prayer and affective prayer. The person has reflected on the way of discipleship and its call to **moral living** and to consideration for other persons; the person has found enough similarity with Jesus to be able to **meet** him in prayer and to **desire** to know, love and follow him; the person's **feelings** have come into prayer, feelings of love and of sorrow, feelings of desire and of resistance; the person is beginning to face the **cost** of discipleship and to put **order** on his/her life in tune with the values of Jesus. **More of heart** and less of thought features in his/her prayer. As a result of this development, **less material** is holding her in prolonged attention on God. For instance, the word 'come' is enough to hold her in simple attention on the Lord. Prayer is **shifting** down deeper into **attitude and desire**, such as, the attitude of wanting to be with Jesus, of wanting to do God's will, of wanting to be unselfish, etc. There is a **shift** to a level **deeper** than feelings; it is a shift to **commitment** and consistency.

Transition

A **definite transition** can occur at this stage, and it takes the form of **dryness**. **Words** in prayer feel like "just words, words, and words." **Thoughts** are no help for holding the person in prayer. **Feelings,** too, have become dried up. Yet, there is **strong desire** for God and for God's will, but no feeling of satisfaction **during** prayer.

The experience

The **experience** of prayer is one of **helplessness**, non-control, disarray. There is **anxiety** about prayer itself, and **anxiety** about doing God's will in general. There is a sense of **failure** in prayer and a temptation to give it up as a hopeless effort. One's **imagination** is all over the place when one **sets oneself** to pray, and these 'distractions' are unsought and unwanted, but can't be controlled; one cannot **focus** one's thoughts on God. All one can do is **want God**, but that is without the former consolations of God. Efforts to return to **earlier fervour** in prayer all end in failure. The **longing** for God continues, but one **doesn't understand** what is happening or why.

Spiritual Direction

This is a crucial stage for spiritual direction, from some director who will help the pray-er to **interpret** what is going on and to **cooperate** with what God is doing. The person knows somehow on the **inside** that things are okay despite the disappointing experience, but he/she needs the **outer** word from someone to match that "**inner** word".

What does a director do?

A director pays attention to what is happening **outside** of prayer as well as what is happening **inside** the prayer, for the outside and inside must match. "By their fruits you will know them." (*Matt* 7:16)

Outside of prayer

You have become aware of the person's faith **history**. She/he has got to know Jesus and the cost of discipleship; has been meeting Jesus in loving friendship in prayer; has grown less self-seeking, more unselfish; is able to be there for others for their sake; has grown enough in self-knowledge to be realistic about self; and so on. This person is living at a level of **commitment** and beyond personal whim. There is personal depth. He/she is able to do without nice feelings. So, the indications are that this dryness is **positive**.

The Prayer itself: how are you to **interpret** it?

Prayer has descended to another level, from relating **through** the senses to relating **without** the senses; it is the level of **faith**. On one level there are 'distractions'; but the prayer is at the **deeper** level in the form of **desire** for God, wanting God, surrender to what God wants.

Prayer is now an **attitude**, not a mental focus. No **focus** carries the relationship, for the level of the senses is bypassed. Prayer is at the level of intellect and will. God is presenting himself **as spirit** to the person's spiritual faculties of intellect and will, **directly**. The **imagination** is moving randomly, because the person is awake, but these **involuntary** distractions on the surface are not taking the person away from God.

The two levels, of sense and of faith, have become distinct and evident.

Interpretation

- ❦ There is a shift **from** senses **to** faith.
- ❦ The **helplessness** on my part means that God is more in control.
- ❦ **Distractions** are only apparent, and not taking me from God, for the prayer is somewhere else.
- ❦ I need to shift from my older idea of "success" in prayer.

- ❦ I am to **move** from wanting the consolations of God to wanting the God of consolation.
- ❦ I give up wanting to see myself as "successful" at prayer.
- ❦ In prayer there is "a secret inflow of loving wisdom" from God. (St John of the Cross)
- ❦ Prayer is at the level of my **will**.
- ❦ I can't pray: I ask God to do it.
- ❦ My prayer is now at the level of faith: I am called now to **live** also at the level of faith and be led by grace.
- ❦ From now on, if I want to meditate and reflect, I must do it **separately** from dedicated prayer time.

B. Negative dryness

The experience of negative dryness tends to be quite different, and it is not uncommon.

A description
- ❦ Prayer is bland; no interest.
- ❦ Feeling disconnected, not just distracted.
- ❦ I want to avoid prayer.
- ❦ I am up in my head; I am not in touch with feelings.
- ❦ I am in prayer on my own terms.
- ❦ The dryness that is negative may come from deliberate sin.
- ❦ This dryness is quite different.

Director: Helps person to check out on possible **causes**, such as:
- ❦ Focus is more on oneself than on serving God; focused on getting consolation.

- Careless about entry to prayer.
- Avoiding something in his/her life which should be faced up to, thus making the person be out of touch with her/his real self.
- Covering too much text.
- Thinking that prayer is all my work and up to me, in this way blocking God.
- Keeping control.
- Afraid of poverty in prayer; wanting to be sure to have experience in prayer.
- A moral turning away from the Lord.
- If depressed, or in grief.

Chapter 14
Recognising Prayer

When I meet a director or a retreatant for the first time, I listen to his/her account of prayer trying to perceive, if I can, **where** in the person the prayer is taking place. Is it discursive? Is it prayer with use of the imagination? Is it prayer at another level, without use of words or images? Is the prayer a wholly receptive prayer? A spiritual director tries to help a person to pray in the way that the Holy Spirit currently desires that person to pray. For prayer is never a fixed pattern: it is an on-going and developing communication with God. And I want to stand beside the person where he/she is comfortable now with God.

A spiritual director needs to be able to recognise **how** this person is praying so as to be able to support the person's response to the Spirit. Take a few instances:

1. This person likes to linger over the meaning of a word or phrase, such as, "I have called you by name, you are mine", and to reflect on who is saying this, and the implications it bears for her, and the privilege of being singled out and desired, and perhaps resistance to this. It is a discursive way of praying. The thinking can lead her to relating.

2. Another person is able to enter with the imagination into a gospel scene.

3. Yet another person is no longer able to focus with the imagination as formerly, but yet experiences a strong desire for God.

4. Another person is very distracted in prayer and finds it hard to face into prayer and, as a result, often enough neglects it.

5. Another likes just to sit and finds that prayer is

given. It is a simple awareness of God's active presence. It is surrender to God.

6. Yet another finds prayer is dry and bare. It is an attitude of waiting and longing, without felt satisfaction.

How is one to help these persons to pray in the way that the Spirit wants them to pray? To know this, one needs a **broad map** of how prayer tends to develop so as to recognise where on the broad journey of prayer a person may be. A **key question** for this is:

Am I to focus on **what** the person prays with, i.e. the **content**, or am I to focus on **how** the person is praying, i.e. the **level** of prayer?

A Broad Map of Prayer

Three Levels of Awareness
A. **Body**: (bodily faculties):

The level of the senses: The five bodily senses; the interior senses of imagination and memory. These are our sense faculties. This level includes sensory feelings; emotions; moods; pleasure and pain; fear; anger, etc. (We share this level with animals).

B. **Soul**: (spiritual faculties):

The level of intellect & will: These are our spiritual faculties. This level includes our capacity for thinking; desiring; loving; deciding; abstract understanding; our capacity for meaning; for idealism; for commitment.

C. **Spirit**: (beneath intellect & will):

The level of spirit: This level is below our intellect & will. It is our inmost centre; our core; in the Bible, it is called 'heart'. It is the place of decision; the ground of our being. God dwells here.

In our ordinary communication with each other, we use **level A and level B** together.

Three Levels of Prayer
Prayer 1:
> Here we use **level A and level B** together. Examples are: vocal prayer; meditation; imaginative contemplation; affective prayer. In this prayer level, **simplification** happens and then, less mental material carries longer attention on God. But levels A and B are still used together.

Prayer 2:
> Here **level A** is **bypassed** by God. (God alone can bypass level A to communicate with us.) Prayer is now at level B. It is **Prayer of Faith.**

Prayer 3:
> Here **level C** (the inmost centre) arises into awareness. This is the **Transforming Union.**

The Journey of Prayer
Prayer 1

When a relationship grows
The journey of personal prayer is the experience of one who is living a personal faith relationship with the God of Jesus Christ in the Spirit. It may be compared with the relationship between friends. When a relationship between **two friends** grows in intimacy, their way of communicating with each other also grows and goes through changes. There is more truth expressed between them and there is a growing trust; affection is felt and expressed; new levels of communication become possible; there is depth.

It is the **same** with the felt relationship with **God**: according as the lived friendship with God grows, prayer also changes and it *descends to deeper levels.* The truth about self is faced; trust increases; affection is felt and expressed; desire for God and for God's will grows. We note that prayer and the lived relationship interact: the **inner** and the **outer** match each other.

Communication becomes communion
When a relationship between **two friends** grows in intimacy, less needs to be spoken. Small gestures – a word, a look, a touch – convey much more than many words did formerly. *Communication becomes communion.* Being **with** the other can be enough. Even silence becomes more unitive than words, for words can spoil the silent presence to each other when this presence is deep.

Simplification
Similarly, in a growing **faith relationship**, prayer becomes **simple** and deep over time. Where, earlier, a lot of material (e.g. from the gospels or from the Old Testament) was needed to hold one in prolonged attention on the Lord, now less material is required. A word or a phrase becomes enough to hold one's **loving attention** for longer periods. Prayer becomes **affective**: love for the Lord is felt and expressed. Just **a little amount of material** is needed to carry the simple communication between the person and God. **Prayer becomes simplified.** This communication is two-way. It is becoming evident already that God is **active** in this prayer: it is because God is active that only a little amount of material is enough for holding the person now in prolonged attention on God. The person is like someone in a canoe being **carried** on the flow of a stream, needing to do very little to keep the communication going.

A shift to attitude
What comes to the fore now is the *level of attitude* present in praying. The connection with the Lord is still being carried by the small amount of material being focused on, but the level of attitude becomes more and more significant. Attitudes such as love, desire, self-giving, trust, wanting to do God's will, openness

to receiving God's love, closeness to Jesus, feature more and more in one's awareness.

How, more than What

This kind of prayer is harder to report on because less can be said about it and maybe less is noticed. Where formerly one could describe how, say, one interacted with Jesus who was meeting with Bartimaeus, the blind beggar in Mark 10, now, at this stage, the prayer is more like a **state of relationship**. For instance, I may be more aware of being looked at by Jesus: I may be caught into love and wonder. There is still some mental or imaginative content carrying the person's prayer. Note that the prayer time is more about **how** one is praying than about **what** one is praying on: the emphasis has moved from the **content** of the prayer to the *level of engagement* in prayer.

All this time, it was *Prayer 1* that was happening: **level A** and **level B** were going on **together**.

Prayer 2

Transition: Going deeper still

A definite transition now takes place and contemplative prayer begins. It is the **beginning** of the *Prayer of Faith*. This transition happens when the bodily dimension, by which I mean words, images, ideas, feelings, **no longer carry** the communication between God and the person. Prayer has dropped down to another **level** in the person. God's action is now **bypassing** the normal human processes of communication that we use to communicate with one another and is addressing the person at the **deeper level** of intellect and will; God, as Spirit, is directly meeting the human spirit. Only God can do this. This is contemplation, but not imaginative contemplation. St John of the Cross speaks of God's part here as *"a secret inflow of loving wisdom"*, "wisdom" drawing the intellect, and "love" drawing the will, and "secret" because the senses cannot pick this up. Prayer feels **arid, dry**, for the level of the **senses** is being bypassed. The senses do not have a part to play in receiving God's communication; they are displaced, so, it is a very **painful** time.

Night of the Senses

It is the **Night of the Senses**, a night as regards the senses for they cannot pick up the **light** that is shining directly into the intellect and will. Prayer now is not happening at the level of words, images, ideas, feelings. The person has to learn to **let go** of the old familiar ways.

Prayer of Faith

Neither words nor images are able now to carry the prayer relationship. Words in prayer feel like "just words, words, and words." There is attentiveness at **one** level and distractions at **another** level. Prayer feels like being in a cinema but one doesn't know where the screen is. Prayer is now love, desire, a wanting God, a wanting to surrender. Prayer is at the level of my **will**. Prayer feels like a **waiting**, or like a **listening** for a sound at the edge of hearing, barely audible. Prayer now is **received**; it is **done** to one; it is **a loving surrender**, which as yet is unable to become full surrender. There is a **striving**. "Obscurity" describes it better than "darkness", for there **is** some kind of light. It feels like one is in a **trackless desert**, in unknown territory, on uncharted waters. "I don't know where I am; have I gone backwards?" It is an important time for seeking **spiritual direction**. There is a temptation to give up prayer; and yet an inexplicable longing for prayer. "I stay with prayer even though it feels like failure; I stay because God deserves my time." The helplessness becomes something good when it drives me onto God.

Involuntary distractions

One's **imagination** is still active, because one is **awake**, but imagination is now **random** during prayer, moving hither and thither, out of control. Prayer feels like **disarray**. The imagination's waywardness can take away one's satisfaction in prayer. One must learn to accept as good the prayer one is being given, and even to accept feeling poor in prayer. One may quieten the surface of the mind with the gentle use of a word or a mantra, but the prayer itself is at another level.

These distractions are **involuntary**, and are not really interfering with the prayer. In fact, according to Dom John Chapman, one must **want** the involuntary distractions to be there, for they are part of having a body, and so in saying "yes" to their presence one is saying a "yes" to being human: we are **embodied** spirits.[46]

Surrendering control
It is, as I said, a painful time **until** one eventually stops fighting against the change that has happened. It is part of the long journey of surrendering control and making room for the Lord. It is worth keeping in mind that this **surrender** is to a Person, the Lord. There is love here. Surrender is growing, by God's gift. Control is gradually being taken from the person **in** prayer; this is also happening **outside** of prayer.

Shadow side
The light that is coming in is seen **indirectly** in the growing realisation of *one's shadow side* – all the self-interest that is operative in the person, both in prayer and outside of prayer.

Here the lid is off the **subconscious** during prayer, and unresolved issues from the **past** now surface in order to be suffered and accepted and healed. With so much hidden light coming in, there is a great increase in *self-knowledge*; this light reveals so much self-interest, and so much mixture of motivation. "*Who will deliver me from my ego-self?*" One sees oneself as a sinner and as needing a Saviour. Here one needs to hold **two truths** together: **God loves me**, *and* I **am a sinner**. I face my basic need for salvation: I cannot save myself. St John of the Cross writes of the purification of **memory** so that I become better able to be in the present moment. This is a preparation for intimacy with the Lord, for all intimacy is present-moment-ness.

Helpless

I feel, however, that I cannot pray and so I ask God to pray in me. Prayer is **dry**, but I find that things are worse if I don't pray. I **need** this prayer, whatever it is. I pray out of need now, not out of joy. Attempts **to regain control** by resorting to former methods won't succeed. Since thinking **interferes** with full prayer, I do my meditating and reflecting **outside** of full prayer. Because my **emotions** are bypassed in this prayer of faith and so don't have any share in the hidden love that is going on, I need some **spiritual reading** in which I find savour and satisfaction for my emotions.

Outside of prayer

I **pray** at the level of FAITH: I am called now to **live** also at the level of FAITH, and to be led by grace, choosing to be like Jesus, and to make him my reason for choosing and acting. **Outside** of prayer, there is a deepening of commitment. There is a **deeper loving** because there is a dying to one's ego-self. There is a growing patience with self and with one's limitations. The arena of growth is likely to be in the 'market-place'; growth in prayer will follow, if not blocked.

This *Night of Faith* is also known by other names: St Teresa of Avila: Prayer of Quiet (4th Mansions) and Prayer of Union (5th and 6th Mansions); St John of the Cross: Dark Night of the Senses and of the Spirit; Ruth Burrows: 2nd Island (in *Guidelines for Mystical Prayer*).

Night of Spirit

The whole purification process goes even deeper in the **Night of Spirit**. God's loving inflow is exposing one's **motivations** and purifying them. The purification is passive, done in the person by the loving action of God. The Lord is leading the person to being in prayer and in a lived relationship, **less for self** and more for God. Prayer becomes a further drawing away from self-centredness and self-interest to a real love in the way that God loves. Old securities are taken away to make space for an ever deeper **trust**, relying not on oneself but on who God is. **Self-image** as someone good and holy and as spiritually successful is being taken away so that one can rely on **who God is** in himself as loving, merciful and utterly trustworthy. **Faith** is deepened, becoming able to do without perceptible echoes in prayer. There is more **surrender** to God's control of one's praying and of one's daily life. One is brought into reliance on **God's mercy**, and to seeing one's ultimate salvation as an **unearned gift**, not as a reward; seeing it as God's achievement in me, not mine. On his Cross, Jesus said, *"Father, into your hands I commit my spirit."* My life, too, is in God's hands, so I trust. Life's ups and downs conspire, in God's providence, to lead me away from **identifying myself** with what I have and with people's approval of me, so that **my treasure** will lie in what I am in my core – God's beloved child – and resting in his approval is enough. Prayer during this time can feel like merely surviving, hanging in there, desperately trusting in the Lord's love and mercy.

Prayer 3

Transforming Union

At some point, in God's own time, **greater surrender** is given and the person becomes aware that something **deeper** is happening. The heart, the innermost **core** of one's being, comes into awareness. There is a **definite transition** here. The impression now is that prayer is something done in oneself, in this deep place, by **Another**. The prayer now is all God's work, so much so that **trying** to make prayer blocks prayer. This is because trying is a taking back of some control. St Teresa of Avila speaks of God *"waking up in the innermost centre"* (*Interior Castle*, 7th Mansion). André Louf speaks of prayer *"welling up"* (*Teach Us to Pray*).

A new journey

A new journey has now begun, and a further purification. St John of the Cross calls this prayer a "Transforming Union", not a "transformed union", for God's work is not done yet. St Teresa of Avila speaks of the "Spiritual Marriage" (7th Mansions). Ruth Burrows will speak of it as the "Third Island". This is a wholly **receptive** and passive prayer. Prayer can be perceived as going on while the mind is not fully engaged with something else. The level of spirit is a deep, deep place. Sometimes the person can pick up in bodily awareness a sense of **deep touch,** happening at the level of spirit, that reveals the enormous depth that is there. Sometimes the surface of oneself can be drawn inwards down towards the deep centre in great **absorption**, and quiet silence. Sometimes one can become **lost to oneself**, into an unawareness of self as praying.

Congruence

Outside of prayer, there is now likely to be an **authenticity** about this person; there is congruence or matching between the inner self and outer presented image: "What you see is what you get". Ego-self has been faced up to very much. A lot of integration has come about. The depth of intimacy with God goes hand in hand with a capacity for intimacy with friends.

Serenity

The late Carmelite scholar, Noel Dermot O'Donoghue, has named this space "the abode of peace". This would mean that there is a deep peace, but not that there are no troubles or anxieties at the surface. There is a great **sensitivity** now to spiritual consolation and desolation, that is, to the movements of the Holy Spirit and of the destructive spirit. God is asking a **continual "yes"** to the *Paschal Mystery*, that is, to dying to self every day for Jesus' sake. **Daily life** continues to be ordinary, but below the surface it is extraordinary. Fruitfulness is evident: God is working through this person. This person is being drawn into a **total surrender**, such as that described in 1983 by Fr Pedro Arrupe, as already quoted in chapters one and eleven.

Growth in Prayer

Three Levels of Awareness

A. Body: (bodily faculties): Level of the senses; feeling; imagination; memory; pleasure/pain.

B. Soul: (spiritual faculties): Level of thinking & desiring; abstract understanding; idealism; commitment.

C. Spirit: (beneath intellect & will): inmost centre; core; 'heart'; place of decision; ground of our being; God dwells here.

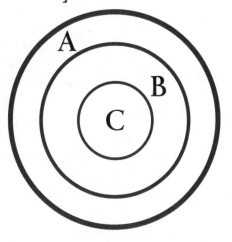

Prayer One:

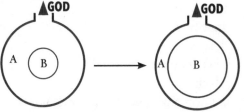

Simplification:
less of **A**
carrying more of **B**

"The soul lives in God": reaching outwards

Prayer Two:

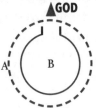

Transition to Prayer of Faith:
A is bypassed ... dryness
Prayer of Faith, Prayer of Union.
A received prayer

"The soul lives in God": reaching outwards

Prayer Three:

Transforming Union:
Inmost centre surfaces into
awareness, indirectly.
A received prayer

"God lives in the soul."

Chapter 15

Anamchara

(A reprint from *The Way*)

A Reflection on giving Spiritual Direction[47]

Beginnings

It was only after I had given my first directed retreat, about four years ago, that I felt I knew what to do in spiritual direction. Before that, I had tried helping some others with their praying, but was not quite sure where to go. But in the course of that retreat I saw development in praying. I found I was able to discern what was significant in retreatants' accounts of their praying: the point where the Lord's action was touching or moving them, and whither he was drawing them. By keeping them in contact with that experience, keeping their noses to the scent, as it were, I found that the inner movement was quite strong and could see the direction in which it was heading.

A second thing I noted was that the person's *way of praying* was, in a way, more important than the subject-matter. Of course, the style of one's prayer is easier to read during a retreat than outside of it. I believe that if a person is faithful to the manner of praying which is at this time appropriate, the Lord's contact and leading will be deeper. But most people need affirmation about this when prayer is becoming simple and when the matter on which they may focus is slight or even nil.

I noted a third thing: there is a prayer of faith or union in which the person opens out to God in surrender. Here there is no focus on definite material; here is the time when the reflection or meditation on texts needs to be done *outside* of the times of full, open prayer. Meditation is still necessary, but not during formal prayer. The material which exercises attraction may indeed come up into the prayer, but when it does so, it comes involuntarily and as part of the movement of surrender.

I noticed too, that the call of God during retreat tends to be towards the cross, towards self-surrender, towards a dying to self in order to be centred on God.

Having noticed all this, I felt I knew the broad lines of how to be helpful to a person outside of retreat.

Annual retreat

While I am speaking about retreats, I want to stress here a point that I think important: it seems to me that one's annual retreat points towards the future and needs to be lived out in the course of the succeeding year. For example, if one has entered a new stage of praying, this has to settle down; or if a self-offering has been drawn from one during retreat, this is going to be asked for in the daily life-experience; or perhaps during retreat one was moved most deeply when one accepted the words, "You are mine"; or when one turned away from self-preoccupation to "look" at God; or when one faced into the word, "Let him deny himself". Such an experience may well describe the programme for the succeeding year. In the annual retreat, one is given a glimpse of the future.

Experience

The experience I reflect upon in what follows was gained not only in directed retreats given, but also, and mainly, in meeting people regularly over these last few years. I see more than a dozen people — mainly men — on a regular basis, i.e. about every three weeks. I go out to meet and chat individually with about a dozen novices — also men — almost every two months. I meet about another dozen people less regularly, and I reply to a number of letters.

Anamchara

It seems to me that a spiritual director is, to use an Irish word, an 'anamchara', which means a soul-friend; he is a companion on another's inner journey *with* and *to* God. He is a companion because both he and the other are on the same quest; and, as a companion, he befriends by listening supportively as the other unfolds his inner story. It is a journey *with* God, because the other has already been found by God, and yet also *to* God, in the sense that the relationship with God calls to grow in depth. And growth is entry into the dispositions of Jesus Christ, and letting him re-live in us his human experience.

Two levels in Christ's experience: the pattern for us

The experience which Christ had on the cross seems to me to be crucial for understanding the way forward. What he went through there was, from a merely natural and superficial viewpoint, utterly meaningless and quite wrong. But, at another level, he was finding there his Father and the risen life: in his lowest experience, he found the high-point of his life; where there was absolutely nothing for self, there he put pure love; in the mud, he found gold; in the ultimate defeat, he found ultimate victory.

All this is so because there are two levels, the experiential and the spiritual: that of the senses, and that of the spirit. It is also the sacramental principle: the bread-and-wine and the presence they carry. This seems to me to run through all our experience in our journey with and to God. It is central to our quest for God in all our activities, for the Creator is hidden in all that he sustains in existence. Jesus found his Father – or should I say was found by his Father? – in the apparent defeat of Calvary.

Prayer

The two levels are evident both in the growth of prayer and in the "market-place".

When prayer moves into simplicity, there is a minimum focus which carries something greater: for example, some fascination with the phrase "Jesus touched them" carries a loving attention to God, which is much greater and wider than the meaning of those words. The praying person needs some contact-point to hold her in the relationship. It is a prayer of recollection. There is an awareness of horizon, but as yet she needs some particular focus.

When the prayer moves beyond that stage, an attempt to focus seems to interfere with the relationship: in order to be in contact with God, one needs to be out of contact with anything definite, one must let go, one must float. The imagination – and hence the ability to think – cannot now contribute: the imagination becomes random, and it occupies itself with all sorts of flotsam and jetsam, while at a deeper level the person is being engaged by God; there are two levels. But at first it seems wrong. Control has been lost. It is a mystical prayer. God is presenting himself as spirit to the spiritual faculties, by-passing the imagination. Aridity is the pain experienced by the person as fantasy tries in vain to follow down into the level of intellect in an attempt to participate in what is going on there in that spiritual faculty. One feels that one has gone backwards.

This is a crucial stage for direction. The praying person needs affirmation, the assurance that all is well. A like simplicity should be evident in such a person's daily living: a desire for God's will, perhaps an anxiety in this desire; an awareness of one's unholiness, of one's inadequate response to God, and yet a peace deep down.

A person may experience a transition here into an ease with this kind of praying, a sense that surrender into it has been given: this is a prayer of union. The two levels are evident. I would hold that the two levels *should* be there: a level of "distractions", so-called, and on another level something else, a kind of engagement, a sense of being happy to be in this somewhat messy state.

Such a person is like a mother who is attending to her guest in the front room, while upstairs the children are running about: if she wants to quieten the children, she has to abandon her guest; if she stays with her guest, she has to put up with the noise upstairs. The imagination is now like those children: it will not stay quiet.

The random activity of the fantasy is evidence that one is

awake: that is all. I am distrustful of a search for one-pointed-ness: this is like trying to regain control. But when the imagination is random, one is more under the Lord's control: and that is really what is desirable. One may at times be drawn into mystery, but in my opinion such absorption should not be engineered by any technique, such as the use of a mantra: it should be left to the Lord to do it, whenever it pleases him.

People who pray like this recognise that although during the time of prayer nothing much seemed to be going on, apart from the superficial flow of random fantasies, they are certain, during the rest of the day, that something was received which is empowering them to cope with their situation and to be patient, spontaneously unselfish, and able to let go of their plans when an unexpected request intrudes: there is surrender of self in prayer and in life.

To describe the prayer, the word "obscurity" is preferable to "darkness", which seems too strong a word, for there is some light: people may refer to it as a "benign darkness", a sense of inner poverty, a sense of being "engaged" or even of being "held", a sense of being "enfolded" by some mysterious Lover; there is an at-home-ness with mystery. The experience can resemble "peripheral vision": you know you are aware of something at the edge, but it eludes direct focus.

There can be a harmony or uneventfulness in such prayer, which is like the experience of putting one's hand into water of the same temperature as one's hand, without looking: you do not know whether you are in it or not. This harmony is a good sign. Nothing much can be reported about such a prayer-experience, except that there is a certain variation in it, some life, and eventually a varying intensity, a sense that the imagination is sometimes more stilled, and this not by one's own doing: there may be a degree of absorption. The conversation with the spiritual director at this stage is likely to centre much more on life outside of prayer: the attempt to surrender to God's will in one's circumstances.

Prayer may develop further: the touches of union with God may deepen, God drawing the intellect deep into himself in mystery, thus engaging the whole self in a very strong intensity, which captivates the faculties of sense as well as spirit. God is preparing the person for the transforming union in which his "access" to the person, or rather interaction, will be below the level of the faculties, deep within the spirit, where he will dwell and awaken.

But life-experiences may at this stage be bitter. The two levels are there again: God is at work detaching the person from all that is not God, so as to take her ever more deeply to himself; he is calling forth total surrender; he is emptying out a space for himself by displacing the self. Love, by excessive love, is preparing his own abode.

Prayer and life

Growth in contemplative or mystical prayer is an aspect of the person's growth *outside* of prayer. Prayer now will not be helped by technique – the time for techniques is past – but only by a co-operation with the Lord *within* prayer, by allowing the awareness of "whatever it is" to be vague, undefined, general; and by the effort *outside* of prayer to be Christ-like in relation to one's tasks and the people one deals with. The growth of the prayer hinges very definitely on the growth in oneself as a person; development in the prayer will be the echo of the development in being; what matters is the kind of person you become.

Differences

How that personal growth is *reflected* in one's consciousness during formal prayer will depend on one's temperament. So two individuals, different in temperament but, let us suppose, equally close to Christ and his Father, will experience this closeness differently in accord with their make-up. Thus, one, outward-looking, more inclined towards action, may be almost unable to perceive inner change during prayer and consequently find prayer almost unreportable; another, inward-looking, less at home with action, sensitive, and perhaps made more sensitive by painful experiences, will be very conscious of the interplay between self and God in the imageless prayer. Both will receive God's consolation, but in the second type it will register with more variation. Thus the difference will not be one of grace or of standing with the Lord, but one of personality type. Hence, what I would say about various kinds of experience in prayer is that they ought to be accepted but not over-valued. God *is* indeed dealing with the individual, making known his love, calling forth a response; but one must not measure holiness by what is perceived within; simply be grateful for God's perceived touch of love, and respond.

Overflow

This brings me to the notion of overflow or echo in mystical prayer. People whose prayer is imageless speak from time to time, especially during retreat, of an image seen during prayer. It may be of a path leading away to a bend and out of sight, or of a boat on the sea, or of being washed up on an island, or it may be a vision of Christ embracing oneself, or of being nailed with him: it can be a sudden flash barely glimpsed, or it can be an extended beholding. The union with Christ is going on *unseen* in the depths, and a symbolic image – or it could be a word – is thrown up from the depths to the surface consciousness. The function of the vision is to reveal to the person what is going on unseen in the relationship, and to give reassurance and elicit cooperation. I have noticed that this is particularly true of a vision of Christ: the experience going on within in the spirit can be too terrifying and awesome – he is the Lord – and so the vision is needed to reassure the person that all is well and that the reaction experienced is the effect of Christ's closeness in a spiritual way to the person's spirit. The real thing is below words and images: these are merely an overflow or echo of it. For we do not experience God directly: it is the self's reaction to God's deeper action that is experienced. So experience of God is only *indirect*.

The director's role

What goes on in a consultation? My experience is that the spiritual director's role in it is: *to receive, to point the other on God* and *to affirm.* I will take each heading in turn.

I. To *receive*

As to this first heading, "to receive", I have been particularly helped by the extended article by Fr Bill Connolly SJ, entitled, "Contemporary spiritual direction: scope and principles", in *Studies in the spirituality of Jesuits*, June 1975. He names three areas for discussion in a consultation, and he links them with the words *faith, hope,* and *charity*, and to these I add a fourth: *spiritual reading.*

> a) *Faith*: the relationship with God in prayer: I always ask about prayer, what the experience is like. I help the person to articulate it, and I affirm it and often facilitate it. I must ask about prayer because God's Holy Spirit is the true director: it is to him that I and the person must listen, and it is a person who prays who is sensitive to him, and can hear him and perceive his gentle pressure. Prayer is desire, and like desire it is movement; only when one is in motion can one be conscious enough of attractions and resistances within oneself to a degree that is helpful for discerning God's attracting, so I think that spiritual direction is hardly possible without regular prayer.
>
> b) *Charity*: the relationship with God in one's dealings with one's fellow men and women. The only valid test of prayer – of one's sincerity before God – is how one is living with others. It is in our interaction with others that we are revealed to ourselves; and it is in our struggle to live out Christ's invitation to love and to forgive that we grow as persons. So I always want to hear some-

thing about relationships.

c) *Hope*: desires and difficulties. "Hope" is an approximate but useful word under which to gather comments on the place of desires and difficulties on the inner journey; for hope is about a desired future goal which keeps me going during the present difficulties.

Spiritual direction is about helping someone who *desires* to be a follower of Christ. Without desire, no direction is possible, the person must want something and if there is to be depth, there must be strong desire: only strong desire can keep him going. I am reminded here of the ambitious desire of James and John recounted in Mark 10:35-45: Jesus did not criticise their desire for greatness, he re-directed it.

It is in the *difficulties* which are inevitably part of a follower's experience that his desires are re-directed by the Lord; and it is here, especially, that the two levels I spoke of earlier come into play. In the case of the person whose way of life is, so to speak, in the "market-place", the struggle to grow will be mainly experienced *outside* of prayer as in the case of the teacher coping with the classroom scene; the parent adjusting to the changed relationship with her children as they grow up and apparently away from her; the business of trying to get on with those one lives with and of becoming someone who excludes none and forgives all; coping with the burden of all the unwanted calls on one's time and energies; coping with the sheer weight of living; with failing memory; with one's increasing sense of one's unimportance; with one's decreasing store of physical and psychic energy; with the tension between action and contemplation and so on.

I think that what one has in all one's difficulties is an unwelcome experience of *self*; this is really what gets under one's skin. And as one grows as a person, there is *a losing of control* over one's life and an experience of one's *limits*. The teacher, if he is to become an educator, may have to settle for less external control in the classroom; the parent has to allow the adolescent son or daughter to move into independence; in my community and in my other relationships I have to give up the desire to change others and the desire that they serve my needs. This loss of control, which is really an experience of self being reduced and of desired success becoming unattainable, can be very bitter; and it invites one to search for some meaning and help in the example of Christ as he coped with failure. One must find something *good* in the bitter experience if one is to keep going and continue to be Christian in one's external behaviour and inward attitude; and this is found in the level below the surface. Unless one looks for what Jesus found in Calvary – the Father's will – one will not find (or be found by) the Father and Jesus in one's experience of difficulty. What one means by "success" must undergo change. There is a relentless process of letting-go that is imposed upon one by very ordinary experience. Somehow, if one is to be more and more deeply found by Christ, one must settle for being dragged into a share in his negative experiences; one's expectation of "paradise now" must melt away. Christ cannot take me fully into his union with the Father unless I allow him to take me into his experience of saying "yes" to the realities of human living. Self's desires must be progressively displaced if one is to be filled by Christ and drawn by him into the current of love flowing between him and his Father.

I mentioned above the tension between action and contemplation. In prayer of union or faith, according as the contemplative state expands, people notice that a tension arises between the drawing from within and the business and detail of daily living. Activity which he formerly relished and took in his stride is now experienced as a kind of intrusion. There is an abrasive co-existence of contemplation and the need to act: there is a desire for space in which to be quiet, and yet so much has to be done. Some people may interpret this as a call to a contemplative order, but it is more likely, I think, to be a normal development in one whose vocation is to be a contemplative-in-action. It seems to me that the tension will be sorted out – through God's gift, of course — by wanting God more and more, by one's surrender to him in everything, by an increasing focus on him. There is a progressive attrition of my desire and a deepening surrender to his. Full surrender is experienced as not humanly possible: the final breakthrough in yielding is experienced as gift. No attempt to sort oneself out psychologically — I mean, using this or that method, trying to slow down, or whatever — will resolve the tension between the two lives. The solution lies below the level of mere activity: it lies at the level where self is dispossessed, surrendered, where God takes over, where the person becomes a pliable instrument in his hand. That is what God wants, a pliable instrument, so that the person stays in a real union with God, a union of wills, not only in what he does but in how he does it. The tension is resolved when self-interest is out of the way.

The other part of the unwelcome experience of the self is, of course, the growing sight of one's poor response. Prayer seems to give one a hidden light which shows one how to live as a follower of Christ. This light shows up very obviously in a negative way, revealing that one is not responding in one's life as one should. And I suspect that, if one is honest, one will admit that one never adequately responds to God's call. The final resolution of the tension which this causes is found in recognising that Jesus is my Saviour more profoundly than he is my brother: that my primary relationship with him is as my Saviour (is not 'he-who-saves' the very meaning of his name, 'Jesus'?). He is the one who picks me up if I admit my need of him — and my need is always there. There is always personal poverty, and there is always the Saviour's love; and when the poverty is embraced, welcomed, wanted, the Saviour most deeply finds me and picks me up. If one *thanks* Jesus for one's sin, even — I mean, for its revelation of one's weakness and of one's need of his forgiveness — I think that one finds a special union with him there. St Thérèse of Lisieux implied as much, a year before her death, in a letter (dated 17 September, 1896) to her own sister Marie, where she said, "My desires for martyrdom are nothing... In fact, they are the spiritual riches which make us unjust — when we rest complacently in them... *What pleases him is to see me love my littleness and my poverty, the blind hope I have in his mercy...* That is my sole treasure." What matters, in the end, is not whether I am sure that I love and serve him, but that I am sure that he loves me, no matter what. This, in the end, is what I must cling to: this is all Jesus had on the cross, total focus on the other.

2. *To point the other on God*

It is in helping a person with his difficulties that the director "points the other on God". I notice that people have a constant tendency to try to sort out their struggle without bringing God into it. There *is* a time early on when one's growth is a matter of taking oneself in hand and making the obvious moral effort to bring external behaviour into line with one's duty and, for this, one's resources within seem to be enough. But a time comes when human effort reaches a limit; it is as though one has met a glass wall. One sees ahead to where one ought to be, but one cannot get through. One is now trying to be truly good, seeking a good-ness which is more interior, where motive needs to be purified and instinctive reactions sanctified. At this point, the effort to sort oneself out without reference to God proves sterile. One has to give up clawing at the glass wall and be, as it were, carried over it. Or, to use a different analogy, one is like a bumble-bee trying to get through the upper pane of glass and failing to find the way through until, exhausted from vain effort, it collapses and falls down between the two parts of the window. Former effort is now sterile and one has to collapse into another's arms. The fruitful-ness experienced here seems to me to be the obverse side of the fact that we are essentially made for relationship, that we are not being our true selves when we try to go it alone, when we try to manage without a conscious turning towards God.

Whether or not we acknowledge it, we *are* each already in re-lationship with God in every fibre and molecule of our being, for he is the Creator, sustaining us in existence every second, all the time lovingly involved with us as the giver and sustainer of our every gift. This much we share with all creatures, but we, as creatures who are intelligent and also free, are invited to become *aware* of his involvement with us. Thus, when we relate to God consciously, we are more truly ourselves. When we do that in our difficulties, we gain the wisdom and strength to manage them fruitfully. We discover we can find him even in what is most unwelcome, and we gradually come to value more and more the gold below the surface of our experience, I mean the love he has for us, and in the end this becomes our "sole treasure". Is this not what it means to be in Jesus facing the Father?

3. To affirm

I said that part of the director's role is "to affirm". He is to encourage the follower of Christ, helping her to admit to failure and to accept God's merciful view of her.

Should the director challenge? My view is that it is God who does the challenging. Anyone who is praying regularly, thus desiring God, and who is also trying to face the truth by revealing the inner life to another, will inevitably experience God's invitation from within. I think it may be irreverent to challenge from the outside – how does one know the right moment? But when the challenge comes from within, it is coming at a time when a person is able to see and accept it. God knows the moment of readiness, and he then also gives the strength to act. His challenge comes with an offer of peace and of entry into open spaces. Furthermore, there can be a degree of obscurity about what is really wrong. What I mean is this: I have noticed that one may see that something is wrong in oneself, as for example, that one is impatient or intolerant or envious, and it may take six months to do anything effective about it, because the fault adverted to is but a symptom of something deeper, such as non-acceptance of the limited self God has made. It is this deeper level that has to be attended to: my saying "yes" to God in regard to my own set of limitations will issue in a change on the more obvious level of my dealings with people.

The director may challenge people with questions, such as "do you think you are praying enough?" or, "this experience you have of distance from God when you pray: are there instances outside of prayer where you draw back from what you know you should be doing or are you excluding some people?"

But my experience is that people tend to misinterpret their experience, they misread as bad what really is good; they think something is wrong when, in fact, all is well. They misinterpret aridity; or when God's obscure presence is very strong outside of prayer, they can feel a great weight which leads them to think they are suffering from depression. Or they can feel they have gone back to square one when closeness to God has given them light to see more clearly their impurity of motive and their refusals to love and their envy of the good they see in others. When they get some understanding of the good that is going on in their own selves, they can cooperate with God's work on them.

Spiritual reading

Under the heading "to receive", I listed three areas for discussion in a consultation, namely, "faith, charity and hope", and now I want to take up the fourth area I mentioned there — "spiritual reading". I believe it to be very important, and I always ask about it. By "spiritual", I do not mean just any spiritual book; I mean the reading in which *this* person is finding *relish now*, not instruction or information, but delight, savour. The instruction and savour may at times coincide, but it is the experience of savour that defines for me that it is spiritual reading now for this person. The book that gave relish once may not appeal to the heart a year later. This is especially true when full prayer has become *inarticulate*, I mean, beyond the use of words or images. At this stage of prayer, spiritual reading as defined above is vital.

What I think is going on is this: the prayer being inarticulate, the emotions and fantasy can have no direct part in it. But the emotions and fantasy are yearning for some participation in the person's involvement with the hidden, unimaginable God; and it is in spiritual reading that they find this, and they *need* to have it. The reading in which one finds relish articulates a relationship which, in prayer, is inarticulate: in the reading, we hear what we already know but is hidden. Through reading, the levels of the self that are being by-passed by God's action get involved and are satisfied, and so the whole self is drawn into God's attraction. Unless such a person finds this relish through reading, she will be trying, in prayer, to get a glimpse of what is going on out-of-sight, will try to contribute something to the praying, will cling to consolation or try to revive it, will want to have something to report on about the prayer: all this, instead of remaining receptive and open and vague.

I have noticed, though, that a time comes when spiritual reading is not experienced as a need. The person feels fed from within. There is within her a well of peace, a deep well of living water. This is so when prayer has become established at the level of spirit, by-passing not only the fantasy, as earlier, but also the intellect. It is not experienced as coming from outside, but as welling up from within: the self's intensity is gone; it is Another's that is felt. Prayer seems to have no beginning or end: all that one needs for one to be aware of this fountain is idleness. The intellect is free: the prayer – it is Another's – goes on without its necessary involvement; and if the intellect does get absorbed, this is an overflow effect of what is going on beneath it.

So, the last level to surface to consciousness is the first that was touched by baptismal grace, namely, the person's deepest centre. Such people need no articulation from outside; they are, as it were, being spoken to from within, and are being fed by a well of living water which, at times, becomes a living flame. But deep peace is the most characteristic note; it is the abode of peace; it is the Third Island. Yet, outward living is ordinary, nothing special: the two levels again, the gold hidden in the ore. It is a new beginning, on a new journey that is endless – till death, that is – for God is infinitely deep. Note that this union is termed "transforming", not "transformed", for the One who, like fire, has transformed those he touched is an abyss of infinite depth where the journey of transformation need never cease. This abyss is the embrace of Father and Son who can draw us ever more deeply into their current of love, on and on and on.

Apart from scripture, the authors whom people find helpful as spiritual reading are those who seem to talk about the relationship with God from lived experience of it: they are not simply quoting others, but are speaking from a gift of wisdom.

Examples are: Chapman, *Spiritual Letters*; Ruth Burrows; Thomas Green; *The Cloud of Unknowing*; Julian of Norwich, *Showings*; Peter van Breemen SJ; Carlo Carreto; Henri Nouwen; *The Hermitage Within* (anonymous); St Thérèse of Lisieux, *Collected Letters, Autobiography, Last Conversations*; St John of the Cross; St Teresa of Avila; von Balthasar, *Prayer*; André Louf, *Teach us to Pray*; Abhishiktananda, *Prayer*; Maria Boulding, OSB, *Marked for Life*.

There are two books that I have found particularly helpful on mystical prayer: John Arintero, OP, *The Mystical Evolution*, vol 2 (North Carolina: Tan Books, 1978), and Ruth Burrows, *Guidelines for Mystical Prayer* (London: Sheed and Ward, 1975).

Arintero concentrates on the prayer-experience and its evolution and draws from the mystical tradition of Western Christian spirituality; Ruth Burrows focuses very much on life outside of formal prayer. Taken together they are most helpful.

Ruth Burrows is, in my opinion, excessively hard on experiences within prayer. She is indeed right to impress on us the need for detachment from them, but her concern is so strong that she practically disconnects them from union with God. She is right to *distinguish* the mystical gift, which of itself is hidden and imperceptible, from the overflow, which is perceptible and much less important; but she is not right to give the impression of *disconnecting* the gift from the overflow, for the overflow is something normal. How I see it is this: the human being is a composite of spirit and sense, is inextricably soul-cum-body. Because the praying person is such a union, some overflow from the hidden level of spirit to the perceptible level of the sense faculties would surely be a normal, though not inevitable, occurrence and should be taken account of and given its relative importance. As another Carmelite has remarked, Ruth Burrows omits the role of the faculties. This results in her making no room for consolation: quite un-ignatian. But her account of the lived experience outside of prayer is original, and it demythologises much romantic writing about mysticism and is very healthy and freeing. She has done us a great service and this article is engrained all over by what she has written in *Guidelines*.

In conclusion
I am aware that, in my reflection, I have left some questions not discussed, as for example, how to discern whether one is praying enough, and the problem that some people have with getting down to personal prayer. I have chosen to speak most of all about mystical prayer and mystical life because I have been quite surprised at meeting so much of it – and the whole range of it – in people: it seems to me that it is only waiting to be recognised and encouraged.

Finbarr Lynch SJ

(Endnotes)

1   A'Kempis, Thomas, *The Imitation of Christ*, trans Betty Knott. London & Glasgow: Collins, 1963, 73
2   Bianchi, E, *Words for the Inner Life*. Toronto: Novalis, 2002, 199
3   ibid. 199, emphases mine
4   ibid. 200, emphases mine
5   ibid. 202, emphases mine
6   ibid. 200 quoting Erika Schuchardt, emphasis mine
7   Frankl, V, *Man's Search for Meaning*. London: Rider, 1959, 75.
8   Arrupe, Pedro, *Essential Writings*. Maryknoll, New York: Orbis Books, 2004, 201
9   John Grennan, ODC, "Discerning Contemplative Prayer", in Religious Life Review, (27) 1988, p.8
10 ibid. p.8, emphases mine
11 *Ascent*, II, 14, 2
12 Gallagher, Timothy, *An Ignatian Introduction to Prayer*. New York: Crossroad, 2007, 60-61
13 *Spiritual Exercises*, #106, 107, 108
14 St John of the Cross, Collected Works, trans Kavanaugh OCD & Rodriguez OCD, 1991, Washington, 2 DN 5:1
15 ibid. 1 DN 10:6
16 Chapman, John, *Spiritual Letters*. London: Sheed & Ward, 1989, 180-181
17 Chapman, John, *Spiritual Letters*. London: Sheed & Ward, 1989, 294
18 ibid. emphases mine
19 ibid. 181
20 Quoted in Gerald May, *Simply Sane*. New York: Crossroad, 1994, 53
21 Keating, Thomas, *The Human Condition*. New Jersey: Paulist Press, 1999, 6
22 *The Cloud of Unknowing*, Chapter 6, trans. Wm Johnston SJ. New York: Image Books, 2005, 46
23 ibid.
24 Keating, Thomas, OCSO, *Contemplative Prayer in the Christian Tradition*, America, April 8, 1978, p.281
25 Blaise Arminjon, SJ, *The Cantata of Love*. San Francisco: Ignatius Press, 1983, 61, emphases mine
26 *Spiritual Exercises*, trans George E. Ganss, SJ, St Louis Institute of Jesuit Sources, 1992, #89
27 J.P. de Caussade, *The Sacrament of the Present Moment*. Glasgow: Collins, 1981, 20
28 Iain Matthew, *The Impact of God*. London: Hodder & Stoughton, 1995, 16
29 Cited by Cassian, Coll IX, ch 31
30 André Louf, *Teach Us to Pray*. London: Darton, Longman & Todd, 1974, 13
31 Wm A. Barry & Wm J. Connolly, *The Practice of Spiritual Direction*. New York: The Seabury Press, 1982, 68

32 Taken from my article, *Anamchara*, in *The Way*, January 1986, Vol. 26, 62-63 (www.the way.org.uk.)

33 Taken from my article, *Anamchara*, in *The Way*, January 1986, Vol. 26, 67-68 (www.the way.org.uk.)

34 Martin Laird, *A Sunlit Absence*. Oxford University Press, 2011, 135-151

35 Taken from my book, *When You Pray*. Dublin: Messenger Publications, 2012, 85

36 *The Wound of Love, A Carthusian Miscellany*. London: Darton, Longman & Todd, 1994, 145

37 Ruth Burrows, *Guidelines for Mystical Prayer*. London: Sheed & Ward, 1976, 117

38 St Teresa of Avila, *Interior Castle, 7th Mansions*

39 Jean Pierre de Caussade, SJ, *The Sacrament of the Present Moment*, trans by Kitty Muggeridge. San Francisco: Harper, 1989, 5

40 Dom John Chapman, *Spiritual Letters*. London & New York: Sheed & Ward, 1935, 317

41 Iain Matthew OCD, *The Impact of God*. London: Hodder & Stoughton, 1995, 12

42 Op cit 147

43 Arrupe, Pedro, *Essential Writings*, Maryknoll. New York: Orbis Books, 2004, 201

44 Dom André Louf, O. Cist. *The Cistercian Alternative*. Dublin: Gill & Macmillan, 1983, 73-74, emphasis mine

45 St. Thérèse of Lisieux, *Story of a Soul*, ICS Publications, Washington, DC, 3rd edition, 1996, 219-223

46 Dom John Chapman, *Spiritual Letters*. London & New York: Sheed & Ward, 1935, 294

47 My article from *The Way*, January 1986, Vol.26,62-63 (www.theway.org.uk) with permission.